CBSE Ⓧ 2022

Term II

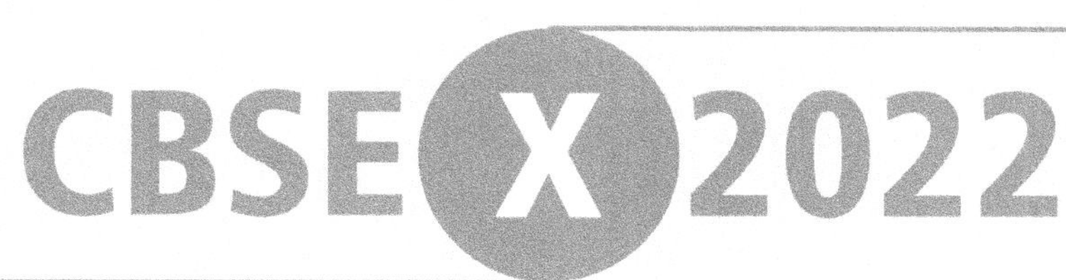

Solved Papers 2011-2020
&
Question Bank

Social Science

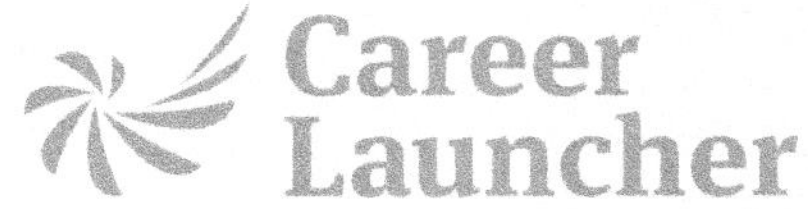

Title   : CBSE Class X 2022 - Term II : Chapter and Topic-wise Solved Papers 2011-2020
                   & Question Bank : Social Science

Language   : English

Editor's Name   : Amit Singh

Copyright ©   : 2022 CLIP

Typeset & Published by :

Career Launcher Infrastructure (P) Ltd.

A-45, Mohan Cooperative Industrial Area, Near Mohan Estate Metro Station, New Delhi - 110044

Marketed by :

G.K. Publications (P) Ltd.

Plot No. 9A, Sector-27A, Mathura Road, Faridabad, Haryana-121003

ISBN   : 978-93-92837-10-4

Printer's Details :

For product information :

Visit *www.gkpublications.com* or email to *gkp@gkpublications.com*

CONTENTS

Unit III : Political Science

Unit IV : Economics

PREFACE

Class X Board Exams are a race against time. You must know how to manage time efficiently if you want to ace your exams. At Career Launcher, we understand the struggle of attempting such a crucial examination for the first time and the pressure that comes along with it. Which is why, our Chapter and Topic-Wise Solved Papers & Question Bank for Social Science for Class Xth Term II have been designed to help you become acquainted with the exam pattern and hone your time management skills, both at the same time.

Exclusively designed for the students of CBSE Class X by highly experienced teachers, the book provides answers to all actual questions of Social Science Board Exams conducted from 2011 to 2020. The solutions have been prepared exactly in coherence with the latest marking pattern; after a careful evaluation of previous year trends of the questions asked in Class X Boards and actual solutions provided by CBSE.

The book follows a three-pronged approach to make your study more focused. The questions are arranged Chapter-wise so that you can begin your preparation with the areas that demand more attention. These are further segmented topic-wise and eventually the break-down is as per the marking scheme. This division will equip you with the ability to gauge which questions require more emphasis and answer accordingly. Apart from this, several value-based questions have also been included.

At the end of the book, solved paper of 2020 Board exam has been provided for you to practice and become familiar with exam pattern.

We hope the book provides the right exposure to Class X students so that you not only ace your Boards but mold a better future for yourself. And as always, Career Launcher's school team is behind you with its experienced gurus to help your career take wings.

Let's face the Boards with more confidence!

Wishing you all the best,

Team CL

Blueprint & Marks Distribution

Social Science Course Structure Term II 2021-22

Theory Paper

		Max. Marks : 40
No.	Units	Marks
I	India and the Contemporary World – I	10
II	Contemporary India – I	10
III	Democratic Politics – I	10
IV	Economic	10
Total		40

Unit 1: India and the Contemporary World - II	
Themes	**Learning Objectives**
Section 1: Events and Processes **2. Nationalism in India** • The First World War, Khilafat and Non - Cooperation • Differing Strands within the Movement • Towards Civil Disobedience • The Sense of Collective Belonging **Section 2: Livelihoods, Economies and Societies** Note: Any one theme of the following. The theme selected should be assessed in the periodic test only and will not be evaluated in the board examination: **3. The Making of a Global World** • The Pre-modern world • The Nineteenth Century (1815-1914) • The Inter war Economy • Rebuilding a World Economy: The Post-War Era **4. The Age of Industrialization** • Before the Industrial Revolution • Hand Labour and Steam Power • Industrialization in the colonies • Factories Come Up • The Peculiarities of Industrial Growth • Market for Goods	• Recognize the characteristics of Indian nationalism through a case study of Non-Cooperation and Civil Disobedience Movement. • Analyze the nature of the diverse social movements of the time. • Familiarize with the writings and ideals of different political groups and individuals. • Appreciate the ideas promoting Pan Indian belongingness. • Show that globalization has a long history and point to the shifts within the process. • Analyze the implication of globalization for local economies. • Discuss how globalization is experienced differently by different social groups. • Familiarize with the Pro- to-Industrial phase and Early - factory system. • Familiarize with the process of industrialization and its impact on labour class. • Enable them to understand industrialization in the colonies with reference to Textile industries.

Unit 2: Contemporary India - II	
Themes	**Learning Objectives**
5. Minerals and Energy Resources • What is a mineral? • Mode of occurrence of Minerals • Ferrous and Non-Ferrous Minerals • Non-Metallic Minerals • Rock Minerals • Conservation of Minerals • Energy Resources o Conventional and Non-Conventional • Conservation of Energy Resources Note: The theoretical aspect of chapter 'Minerals and Energy Resources' to be assessed in the Periodic Tests only and will not be evaluated in Board Examination. However, the map items of this chapter as given in the Map List will be evaluated in Board Examination	• Identify different types of minerals and energy resources and places of their availability • Feel the need for their judicious utilization
6. Manufacturing Industries • Importance of manufacturing • Contribution of Industry to National Economy • Industrial Location • Classification of Industries • Spatial distribution • Industrial pollution and environmental degradation • Control of Environmental Degradation	• Bring out the importance of industries in the national economy as well as understand the regional disparities which resulted due to concentration of industries in some areas. • Discuss the need for a planned industrial development and debate over the role of government towards sustainable development.
7. Life Lines of National Economy • Transport – Roadways, Railways, Pipelines, Waterways, Airways • Communication • International Trade • Tourism as a Trade	• Explain the importance of transport and communication in the ever-shrinking world. • Understand the role of trade and tourism in the economic development of a country.
Unit 3: Democratic Politics - II	
Themes	**Learning Objectives**
6. Political Parties	
	• Analyze party systems in democracies.

• Why do we need Political Parties? • How many Parties should we have? • National Political Parties • State Parties • Challenges to Political Parties • How can Parties be reformed?	• Introduction to major political parties, challenges faced by them and reforms in the country.
7. Outcomes of Democracy • How do we assess democracy's outcomes? • Accountable, responsive and legitimate government • Economic growth and development • Reduction of inequality and poverty • Accommodation of social diversity • Dignity and freedom of the citizens	• Evaluate the functioning of democracies in comparison to alternative forms of governments. • Understand the causes for continuation of democracy in India. • Distinguish between sources of strengths and weaknesses of Indian democracy.

Unit 4: Economics

Themes	Learning Objectives
3. Money and Credit • Money as a medium of exchange • Modern forms of money • Loan activities of Banks • Two different credit situations • Terms of credit • Formal sector credit in India • Self Help Groups for the Poor	• Understand money as an economic concept. • Understand the role of financial institutions from the point of view of day-to-day life.
4. Globalization and the Indian Economy • Production across countries • Interlinking production across countries • Foreign Trade and integration of markets • What is globalization? • Factors that have enabled Globalization • World Trade Organization • Impact of Globalization on India • The Struggle for a fair Globalization	• Explain the working of the Global Economic phenomenon.

Unit I : History

Nationalism in India

Summary

The First World War, Khilafat and Non-Cooperation Movement

- The first world war took place in 1914 and continued till 1918.
- To meet the expenses of war ,tax ,custom duties,were raised.
- Income tax was introduced to breach the economic needs during war time.
- To fulfil the requirement of soldiers, villagers were forced to join.
- Due to various reasons crop failed in 1920 that leads the shortage of food crops.
- In the same time diseases like influenza spread and caused death of peoples.

Khilafat and Non Cooperation Movement

- Disintegration of Ottoman empire was took place after the first world war.
- To uphold the status of Khilafat a movement was started by Muhammad Ali and Shaukat Ali.
- Ali brothers and other Muslim leaders formed a Khilafat committee in Bombay.
- They started Khilafat movement against British empire joining with mass movement started by Gandhiji.
- Gandhiji avails this golden opportunity to unite Hindu-Muslims for freedom struggle.
- In Congress session of Culcutta Gandhiji decide to launch nationwide movement in the support of Khilafat.

Non-Cooperation Movement

- The movement started with the notion of notion of not to cooperate Britishers in every sector.
- Students, teachers, left the educational institutions, foreign goods were boycotted.
- Except madras, the council elections were boycotted.
- Liquor shops picketed, peoples denied to use of foreign cloths.
- In Awadh peasants joined this movement to fulfil their demands i.e to reduce tax, abolish beggar and other social issues.
- They organized Nai dhobi bandh for landlords as a part of social boycott under the leadership of Baba Ramchandra.
- Peasants defined this movement as movement against tax.
- Thousands of plantation workers of Assam left the tea gardens and returned home to support the movement. They took this movement as the movement of land distribution among landless.
- Tribal peasants of accepted this movement as a movement against British policy against forests.
- During this movement the production of textile mills increased rapidly.
- In Awadh peasants expressed their anger on the house of Zamindars and Talukdars.

- The movement had a limited participation and alternatives of British institutions was not available therefore, movement did not attain its goal but contributed in developing the sense Of common people.

Civil Disobedience Movement

- After the failure of Simmon commission, Irwin offered a status of Dominion status and round table discussion. Congress leaders didn't accepted it.

- The demand of Poorna Swarajya or complete independence raised by congress and on 26th of January accepted as Poorna Swarajya Day.

- Gandhiji opted salt to unite the Indian under the umbrella of nationalism to get the goal of freedom.

- Gandhiji gave a ultimatum of eleven demand to lord Irwin to fulfil by 11th of march 1930 and warned him if the government failed to respond he will launch a nation wide movement.

- Lord Irwin didn't responded, Gandhiji started Civil disobedience movement by Salt March.

- On 12th of march Gandhiji started march sabaramati ashram to dandi with his 78 followers.

- Gandhiji covered the Distance of 240 km in 24 day, travelling 24 km per day, by addressing thousands of peoples about Swaraj.

- The salt was defied on the morning of 6th April 1930, by making salt.

- Following Gandhiji, various place of India witnessed the breaking of salt under the leadership of famous freedom fighter.

- Peoples defied to pay taxes like chakidari tax, land tax and also refused to accept forest laws.

- Britisher government started to suppress this nationwide movement relentlessly.

- Brutual repression and peoples aggression compelled Gandhiji to think about the call off the movement and on 5th of march the famous Gandhi-Irwin pact was signed by both.

- According to the pact Gandhiji want to London but his travel to Round Table conference was not successful and he launched the movement again.

People Participation in the Movement

- The participation of all sector was not with the same goal they defined Swaraj as their own mindset.

- The Patidars of Gujarat and Jats of U.P joined this movement to reduce the land revenue but when the movement was stopped they lost their hope.

- The poor landless peasants participated in this movement to remove the land rents.

- The business class joined this movement against British policy regarding trade,as they wanted to earn benefits like during world war.

- G.D Birla and other members of FICCI supported the movement in financial term but with the failure of Round Table Conference they refused to support.

- The worker of Nagpur participated in this movement to oppose the low wages and poor working conditions.

- Thousand of woman took part in this movement by staging agitation, manufacturing salt, picketing foreign cloths but the congress had not clear aspects regarding women.

- This movement had some limits however it was successful in creating a strong sense of Nationalism.

Sense of Collective Belonging

- When the peoples started to identify themselves or all to be part of one nation, than it is said the nationalism is spreading.

- The experience, came from united struggles, created a sense of collective belongings.

- The folklore, folk tales ,popular prints, songs, symbols, history and fiction contributed to create a sense of one or Nationalism.

- To unit people, painters started to visualize India as a mother and a image of mother were portrayed with iron, that invoke peoples to fight against freedom of mother.

- The image of Bharat Mata first created by Bankim Chandra Chattopadhyay later he composed Vande Matram. The song was used in procession or protest against Britishers.

- The reverence for Bharat image is considered as the sign of nationalism and patriotism.

- Folk lore sung by bards in village also relates peoples with the sacrifice and brave heros of freedom movement, which invoke peoples to be a part of freedom movement.

- Images and symbols also contributed in the development of nationalism and create a bond of one nation among peoples.

- Tricolour flag designed in Bengal and flag designed by Gandhiji was example of unifying India by symbols.

- Revival and reinterpretations of history connected peoples with the ancient glory of India and inspired to attain it again by driving out Britishers from India

- These icons, image, history was related with Hindus it also create a sense of alienation among different religions.

Points to know

Nationalism – Notion towards nation.

Forced recruitment – to fulfil the needs of workers or soldiers a imperialist force to join the colonizers.

Satyagraha – Request for truth. Gandhiji used it as a weapon against British empire.

Picket – Blockage of the door to preventing the use of shop or factories by workers or peoples.

Gudem Rebel – A Guerrilla warfare took place in Andhra Pradesh against British empire to achieve swaraj.

Important Personalities

General Dyer – commander of British of army in Amritsar, attacked on the procession of Jaliawala Bagh.

Ali Brothers – Muhammad Ali and Shaukat Ali both brothers organized a committee to oppose the minimization of power of Khilafat.

Baba Ramchandra – Led the peasant revolt in Awadh.

Alluri Sitaram Raju – known as incarnation of god, encouraged the non cooperation movement.

C R Das – founder of Swaraj party.

Muhhamad Ali Zinnah – prominent leader of Muslim League, demanded for the nation of Muslims Or separation of India.

Abanindranath Tagore – famous painter, designed the image of Bharat Mata.

Mahatma Gandhi – started non cooperation, civil disobedience movements based on Satyagraha. He brought Indian under the umbrella of Nationalism to fight against Britishers.

Important Dates

1918-19 – Crops failed in India

1915 – Mahatma Gandhi returned from south Africa in January.

1919 – The Jaliawala Bagh massacre took place on 13th April.

1919 – In march, Khilafat committee was formed.

1909 – Hind swaraj written by Gandhiji was published.

1923 – Non cooperation movement was launched.

1927 – FICCI was formed

1928 – Simon commission was arrived.

1929 – Round table conference took place.

1930 – On 13 march 1930 Gandhiji started salt march.

1931 – 2nd round table conference was held in London.

1931 – Civil disobedience movement was launched.

PREVIOUS YEARS'
EXAMINATION QUESTIONS

▶ 1 Mark Questions

1. **Which one of the following statements is not related to the Gandhi-Irwin Pact?**

    (*a*) Gandhiji agreed not to launch any further mass agitations against the British.

    (*b*) Gandhiji agreed to participate in the Round Table Conference.

   (c) Gandhiji decided to call off the Civil Disobedience Movement.

   (d) The British agreed to release the political prisoners.

[TERM 2, 2011]

2. Why did Nationalists in India tour villages to gather folk songs and legends? Choose the most appropriate reason from the following:

   (a) Nationalists wanted to study their own culture.

   (b) Nationalists wanted to publish it and earn money.

   (c) Nationalists did it because it gave a true picture of traditional culture.

   (d) Nationalists wanted to keep folk culture intact.

[TERM 2, 2011]

3. In which of the following years Mahatma Gandhi inspired the peasants of Champaran district of Bihar to struggle against the oppressive plantation system:

   (a) 1916   (b) 1917

   (c) 1918   (d) 1919

[TERM 2, 2012]

4. In which one of the following Indian National Congress Sessions, the idea of 'Non-Cooperation Movement' was accepted?

   (a) Lahore Session

   (b) Nagpur Session

   (c) Calcutta (Kolkata) Session

   (d) Madras (Chennai) Session

[TERM 2, 2012]

5. The Non-Cooperation Movement began during

   (a) January 1921

   (b) November 1921

   (c) December 1921

   (d) May 1921

[TERM 2, 2013]

6. Name the writer of the book 'Hind Swaraj'.

[TERM 2, 2017]

7. What was the main aim of the popular movement of April 2006, in Nepal?

[TERM 2, 2015]

▷ 2 Mark Questions

8. Two features (1) and (2) are marked in the given political outline map of India. Identify these features with the help of the help of the following information and write their correct names on the lines marked in the map:

   (1) The place, where the Indian National Congress Session of September 1920 was held.

   (2) The place, where the movement of Indigo Planters took place.

[TERM 2, 2011]

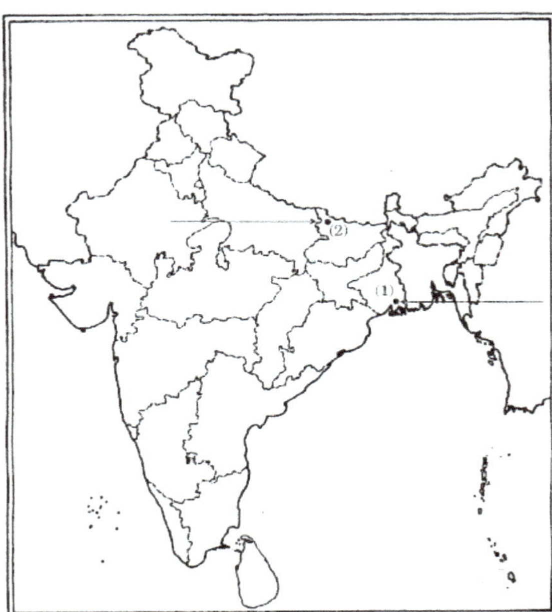

9. Locate and label the following features with appropriate symbols on the same political outline map of India:

   (i) Amritsar: The place of Jallianwala Bagh incident.

   (ii) Bardoli: The place where no tax campaign was held.

[TERM 2, 2011]

10. Two features - A and B are marked in the given political outline map of

India. Identify these features with the help of the following information and write their correct names on the lines marked in the map

(A) The place where Indian National Congress Session was held in September 1920.

(B) The place where the Peasant Satyagraha was held in Gujarat.

[TERM 2, 2012]

11. Locate and label the following items with appropriate symbols on the same map:

(*i*) Chauri-Chaura - The place of calling off the Non-Cooperation Movement (N.C.M.)

(*ii*) Amritsar - The place where Jallian Wala Bagh incident took place.

[TERM 2, 2012]

▶ 3 Mark Questions

12. Explain any three effects of the Non Co-operation Movement on the economy of India.

[TERM 2, 2011]

13. Why did Non-Cooperation Movement gradually slowdown in cities?

Explain any three reasons.

[TERM 2, 2012]

14. How had the First World War created a new economic situation in India? Explain with three examples.

[TERM 2, 2013]

15. How was the Rowlatt Act opposed by the people in India? Explain with examples.

[TERM 2, 2013]

16. Describe the main features of 'Poona Pact'.

[TERM 2, 2015]

17. How did 'Salt March' become an effective tool of resistance against colonialism? Explain.

[TERM 2, 2015]

18. Three features A, B and C are marked on the given political outline map of India (on page 9). Identify these features with the help of the following information and write their correct names on the lines marked in the map:

A. The place where the Indian National Congress Session was held.

B. The place associated with the Peasant's Satyagraha.

C. The place related to calling off the Non-Cooperation Movement.

[TERM 2, 2015]

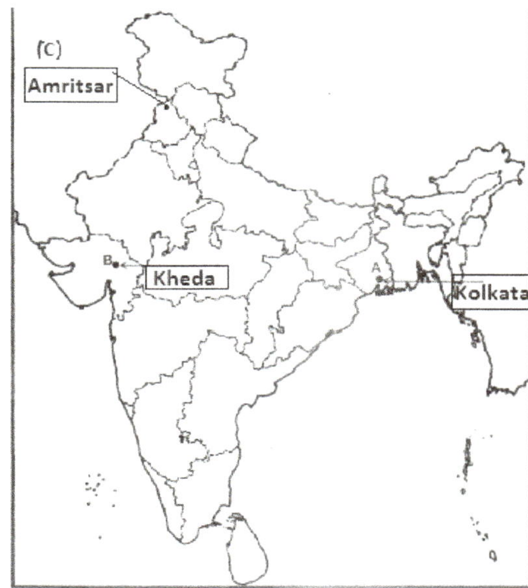

19. (*a*) Name the place where the Indian National Congress Session was held in December 1920.

(*b*) Name the place associated with the movement of Indigo Planters.

(*c*) Name the place related to the Satyagraha of peasants in Gujarat.

[TERM 2, 2015]

20. What type of flag was designed during the 'Swadeshi' Movement' in Bengal? Explain its main features.

[TERM 2, 2016]

21. "The plantation workers in Assam had their own understanding of Mahatma Gandhi and the notion of Swaraj". Support the statement with arguments.

[TERM 2, 2016]

22. Three features A, B and C are marked on the given political outline map of India. Identify these features with the help of the following information and write their correct names on the lines marked in the map:

A. The place where cotton mill workers organized Satyagraha.

B. The place related to the calling off the Non-cooperation Movement.

C. The place where the Indian National Congress Session was held.

[TERM 2, 2016]

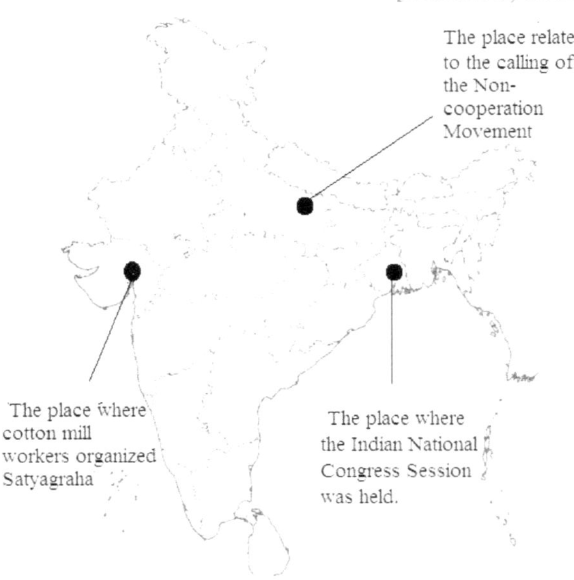

23. Why did Gandhi ji decide to withdraw the 'Non-Cooperation Movement' in February 1922? Explain any three reasons.

[TERM 2, 2017]

24. Evaluate the role of business classes in the 'Civil Disobedience Movement'.

[TERM 2, 2017]

25. Three features A, B and C are marked on the given political outline map of India. Identify these features with the help of the following information and write their correct names on the lines marked on the map:

A. The city associated with the Jallianwala Bagh incident.

B. The place where the Indian National Congress session was held.

C. The place where Gandhiji violated the Salt Law.

[TERM 2, 2017]

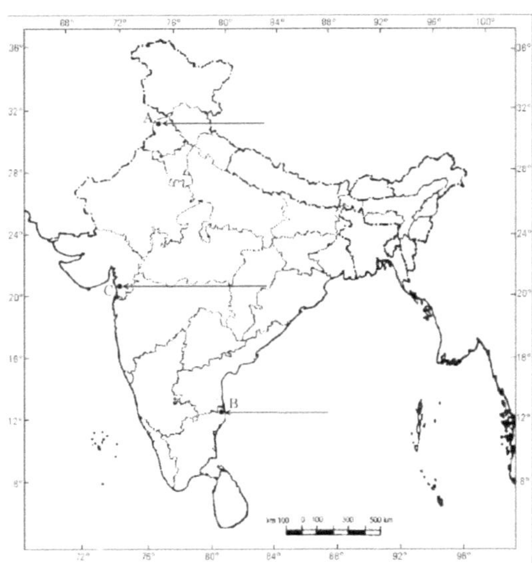

▷ 4 Mark Questions

26. Explain four points about Gandhi ji's idea of 'Satyagraha'.

[TERM 2, 2011]

27. How did people and the colonial government react to the Civil Disobedience Movement? Explain.

[TERM 2, 2012]

▷ 5 Mark Questions

28. Explain the attitude of the Indian merchants and the industrialists towards the 'Civil Disobedience Movement'.

[TERM 2, 2015]

29. How did the Civil Disobedience Movement come into force in various parts of the country? Explain with examples.

[TERM 2, 2016]

30. How did the Colonial Government repress the 'Civil Disobedience Movement'? Explain.

[TERM 2, 2017]

31. Why was Congress reluctant to allow women to hold any position of authority within the organization? How did women participate in Civil Disobedience Movement? Explain.

[DELHI 2018]

⚷ Solutions

1. Gandhiji agreed not to launch any further mass agitations against the British. [1]

2. Nationalists did it because it gave a true picture of traditional culture. [1]

3. 1917 [1]

4. Calcutta (Kolkata) Session [1]

5. May 1921 [1]

6. Hind Swaraj is written by Mahatma Gandhi. [1]

7. Restoration of democracy was the popular movement of April 2006 in Nepal. [1]

8. The features identified are as:

   (1) Calcutta [1]

   (2) Champaran(Bihar) [1]

9. Political outline map of India

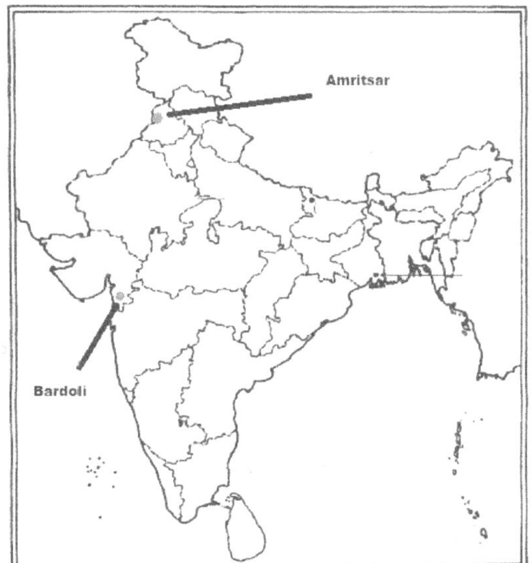

[1 + 1]

10.

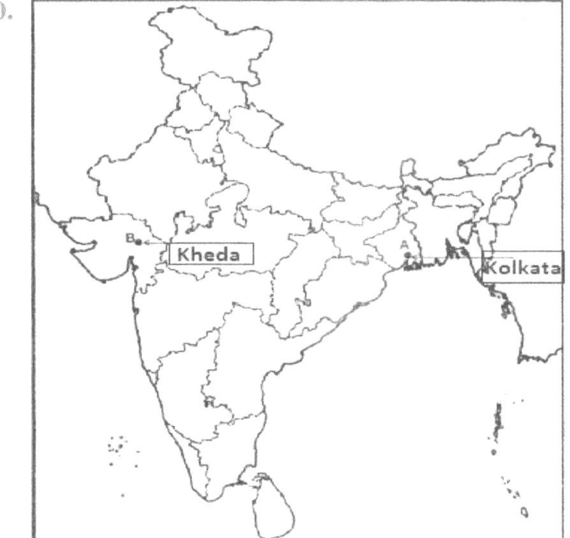

[1 + 1]

11.

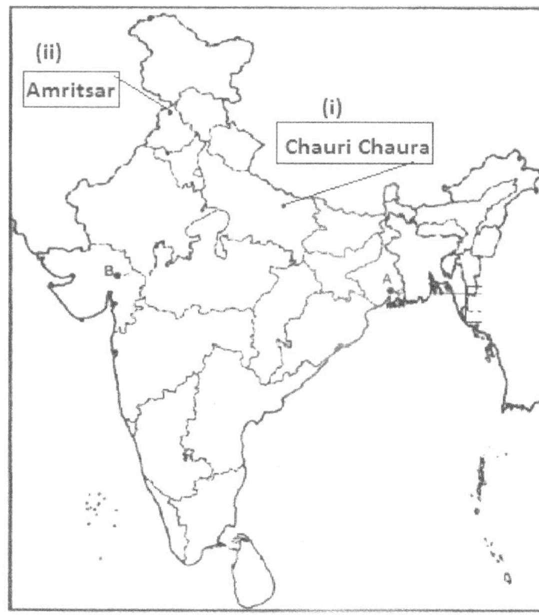

12. The following are the effects of the Non Co-operation Movement on the Indian economy:

   (i) Rejection of foreign goods. Liquor shops were picketed and huge bonfires of foreign clothes were burnt. [1]

   (ii) Between 1921 and 1922, import of foreign clothes halved with its value dropping from Rs. 102 crore to Rs. 57 crore. Many merchants and traders denied to finance the foreign trade and to trade in foreign goods. [1]

   (iii) Indian textile mills and handlooms increased as the people started wearing Indian clothes and rejected the imported ones. [1]

13. The following reasons explains the slowing down of Non-Cooperation Movement in cities:

   (i) Khadi clothes were more expensive than the mass-produced mill cloth, hence people could not afford them. [1]

   (ii) Disruption of the functioning of public institutions caused problems to people as the process of setting up Indian institutions was very slow. [1]

   (iii) Lack of alternate Indian institutions that could replace the British institutions forced the students to go back to their colleges and the lawyers to return back to work in courts thus quitting the Non-Cooperation Movement. [1]

14. The First World War had created huge impact on the economic situation in India.

    (*i*) It led to a huge increase in defence expenditure of British Raj which increased various taxes. [1]

    (*ii*) As Indian industrialists started manufacturing war materials to send to Britain the process of industrialization intensified. [1]

    (*iii*) A demand for industrial goods such as Jute, Bags, Cloth, Rails, etc. increased and it caused a decline of imports from other countries to India and increase in employment in India. [1]

15. The Rowlatt Act of 1919 was opposed in many different ways.

    (*i*) Workers working in railway workshops went on strike. [1]

    (*ii*) All commercial establishments were closed down. [1]

    (*iii*) In different cities rallies were organized.

    (*iv*) The infamous Jallianwala Bagh massacre took place because people had gathered in opposition to the Rowlatt act. [1]

    (*v*) Open fire was ordered by General Dyer, on innocent civilians who gathered outside the city of Amritsar to attend a peaceful meeting.

16. The main attributes of 'Poona Pact' are as follows:

    1. The seats were reserved in provincial and central legislative councils for Schedule Castes but they were to be voted in by the general electorate. [1]

    2. Poona Pact came into acceptance as Gandhiji began a fast unto death. [1]

    3. Ambedkar also accepted Gandhiji's position and Poona pact was announced on September 1932. [1]

17. Salt is a crucial part of food. The dictatorial face of British rule was exposed by the monopoly of tax, salt and government over the salt production. Under this movement, Gandhiji asked for swaraj from Britishers. Mahatma Gandhi started his famous salt march taking 78 of his trusted volunteers along. The march was undertaken from Sabarmati(Gandhiji's ashram) to the coastal town of Gujarat (Dandi) which was over 240 miles. This led to the widespread resistance against British rule. [1 + 1 + 1]

18. (*a*) Kolkata [1]

    (*b*) kheda [1]

    (*c*) Amritsar [1]

19. (*a*) Kolkata [1]

    (*b*) Champaran [1]

    (*c*) Ahmedabad [1]

20. During the Swadeshi movement in Bengal, Flag had become a symbol of defiance. A tricolor flag (red, green, yellow) had been designed. It had eight lotuses symbolizing eight provinces of British India, and a crescent moon, representing Hindus and Muslims. In the meantime by 1921, Gandhiji had designed the Swaraj Flag. It was a tri-color flag (red, green and white) having a spinning wheel in centre, representing the Gandhian Ideal of self help. [1 + 1 + 1]

21. The plantation workers in Assam had their own understanding of Swaraj.

    (*i*) For them freedom meant the right to move freely in and out from their horizons. [1]

    (*ii*) For them it was retaining again to their villages from where they belonged as Under the Inland Emigration act of 1859, they were not allowed to leave tea gardens without permission. [1]

    (*iii*) Thousands of workers left the plantations and headed homes defying the authorities and government of then. [1]

    (*iv*) According to them Gandhi Raj was emerging and their sufferings and troubles would be eliminated. .

22. A. Ahmedabad is the place where cotton mill workers organized Satyagraha. [1]

    B. Chaura Chauri is the place related to the calling off of the Non-cooperation Movement. [1]

    C. Calcutta is the place where the Indian National Congress Session was held. [1]

23. Gandhi ji decided to withdraw the 'Non-Cooperation Movement' in February 1922 due to following reasons: [1]

    (*i*) The Movement was meant to be a peaceful movement but Satyagrahis were turning violent so he felt that Staygrahis needed to be trained properly for mass agitation. [1]

    (*ii*) Congress leaders wanted to contest elections, so they did not want any mass-struggle. [1]

24. Following are the roles of business class in the 'Civil Disobedience Movement':

    (*i*) 'Indian Industrial and Commercial Congress' was formed by the business class in 1920 and the 'Federation of the Indian Chamber of Commerce' and Industries in 1927 to organize business interest. [1]

    (*ii*) Finances were being provided by business class for the movement. [1]

    (*iii*) They refused to sell and buy imported good. [1]

25.

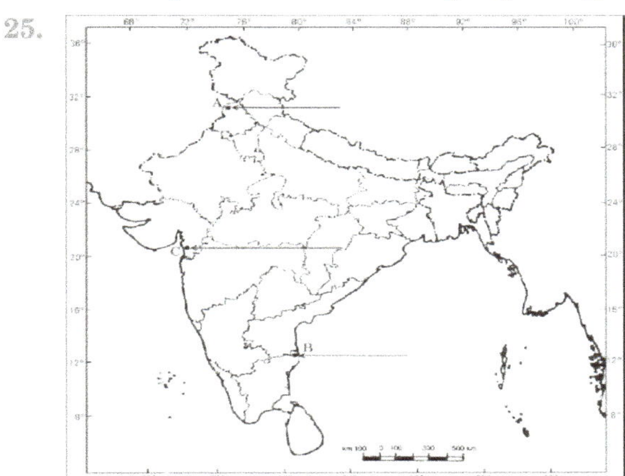

(A) Amritsar [1]

(B) Madras [1]

(C) Dandi [1]

26. The idea of Gandhi ji's Satyagraha can be abstracted as follows:

    (1) It highlights the Power of Truth and the need to search for it. [1]

    (2) It puts forward that if the motive is true and the fight is against the injustice, then physical force is not necessary. [1]

    (3) A Satyagrahi could win the battle through non-violence without being agitated or being aggressive by appealing to the conscience of the oppressors. People need to see and accept the truth, instead of being forced to accept it through the use of violence. [1]

    (4) Gandhi ji believed that truth was bound to ultimately triumph and that 'Dharma' of non-violence was enough to unite all the Indians. [1]

27. People and the colonial government reacted to the Civil Disobedience Movement in the following ways:

Reaction of the people Civil disobedience movement consisted of the people from all castes and classes of the society. [0.5]

    (*i*) Thousands of people from different parts of the country broke the salt law by manufacturing salt and demonstrating in front of the government salt factories. [0.5]

    (*ii*) People boycotted foreign cloth, and protested in front of the liquor shops. [0.5]

    (*iii*) Peasants refused to pay the chaukidari taxes and revenues. Many of the village officials resigned and the forest laws were violated by the forest people by entering the Reserved Forests to collect wood and graze cattle. [0.5]

Reaction of the government The colonial government reacted brtually to stop the Civil disobedience movement by arresting the Congress leaders one by one, Abdul Ghaffar Khan (a staunch follower of Mahatma Gandhi) being one of them. [0.5]

    (*i*) Many were killed by the police firing and the angry crowd had to face the armoured cars. [0.5]

    (*ii*) The government responded with brutal aggression when the industrial workers of Sholapur attacked police posts protesting against Gandhi's imprisonment. [0.5]

    (*iii*) Satyagrahis protesting peacefully were attacked and over 100,000 people were arrested. [0.5]

28. The attitude of the Indian merchants and the industrialists towards the 'Civil Disobedience Movement' can be described as follows:

    (*i*) Indian industrialists believed that the colonial policies were restricting their business as they made huge profits during the First World War. [1]

    (*ii*) They refused to buy or sell any imported goods. [1]

    (*iii*) They were against all the trade barriers and wanted to expand their business at their own. [1]

(*iv*) The organization FICCI (Federation of the Indian chamber of commerce) was organized in 1927, to look after their business interests. [1]

(*v*) They wanted protection against imports of foreign goods and therefore, they were an active participant in the 'Civil Disobedience Movement'. [1]

29. Answer: The Civil Disobedience Movement came into force in various parts of the country as:

(*i*) Gandhiji led the Salt March from Sabarmati Ashram to Dandi with his followers starting the Civil Disobedience Movement. Salt law was broken by most of the people from the different parts of the country. The salt was produced and demonstrated in front of the factories by the people. [1]

(*ii*) The rich Patidars of Gujarat and Jats of Uttar Pradesh in the countryside actively participated in the movement. Many communities were led by these rich peasants, and sometimes they forced the members who were unwilling to participate in the movement. They considered this fight for Swaraj against high revenues. [1]

(*ii*) The industrial working class of Nagpur region participated in the movement. Railway workers, dock workers, coal mine workers took part in the protest rallies and boycott crusade. [1]

(*iv*) Large number of Women also actively participated in the movement. Many came out of their houses, took part in the protest marches and also manufactured salt. [1]

(*v*) Industrialists led by Purshottamdas Thakurdas and G D Birla supported the Civil Disobedience Movement. [1]

30. The Colonial Government took following brutal steps to repress the 'Civil Disobedience Movement':

(*i*) The Congress leaders were arrested by the government one by one. This led to violence in many places of the country. [1]

(*ii*) In April 1930, it arrested Abdul Ghaffar Khan who was a devout disciple of Mahatma Gandhi. [1]

(*iii*) The government arrested Gandhi ji also. [1]

(*iv*) Police fired on an angry crowd in the streets of Peshawar and killed many people. [1]

(*v*) They beat women and children and attacked Satyagrahis. [1]

(*vi*) They arrested about 100 000 people. [1]

31. Congress was reluctant in participation of women-

(*i*) Congress was keen only on the symbolic presence of women within the organization. [1]

(*ii*) Gandhi ji believed that role of women was to look after home and hearth so as being good mothers and good wives. [1]

Participation of women in Civil Disobedience Movement

(*i*) During Gandhiji's Salt March, lots of women came out to participate in protest marches. [0.5]

(*ii*) They manufactured salt and picketed liquor shops. [0.5]

(*iii*) They boycotted foreign goods. [0.5]

(*iv*) Women from high caste families and from rich peasant households participated. [0.5]

(*v*) Moved by Gandhiji's call, they began to see service to nation as a sacred duty of women.

MULTIPLE CHOICE QUESTIONS

1. Mahatma Gandhi travelled to Champaran in Bihar to...........
   (*a*) Understand the geographical extent of India
   (*b*) To encourage people to support Indian goods
   (*c*) Inspire the peasants to struggle against the oppressive plantation system
   (*d*) All of the above

2. Which act gave enormous powers to the British Government to repress political activities?
   (*a*) Irwin Pact
   (*b*) Simon Act
   (*c*) Indian Emigration Act
   (*d*) Rowlatt Act

3. The Simon Commission was not well received in India because......

   (*a*) It did not constitute of any Indian representative

   (*b*) It did not constitute of any women representative

   (*c*) The Indians were not aware of the arrival of the commission

   (*d*) It gave the British absolute cultural rights over India

4. The Salt March or Dandi March was started by Gandhiji on?

   (*a*) 12th March 1936   (*b*) 12th March 1930

   (*c*) 12th May 1930   (*d*) 12th March 1931

5. Why did Gandhiji withdraw the Non-Cooperation Movement?

   (*a*) Gandhiji realized that British was more powerful and could not be defeated

   (*b*) Some Congress leaders wanted to participate in elections to Provincial Councils

   (*c*) Some Congress leaders wanted to lead the movement

   (*d*) Gandhiji felt the movement was turning violent in many places

Answer Keys

  1. (*c*)   2. (*d*)   3. (*a*)   4. (*b*)   5. (*d*)

Solutions

1. Inspire the peasants to struggle against the oppressive plantation system

2. Rowlatt Act

3. It did not constitute of any Indian representative

4. 12th March 1930

5. Gandhiji felt the movement was turning violent in many places

FILL IN THE BLANKS

1. The Khilafat movement was initiated by ____________ and __________.

2. During _______________ movement, the people refused to buy/support British goods.

3. The Jallianwala Bagh incident took place on __________.

4. The ____________ gave Depressed Classes (later to be known as Scheduled Caste) reserved seats in provincial and central legislative councils.

5. This image of Bharat Mata was created by ________________.

Solutions

1. Muhammad Ali and Shaukat Ali

2. Civil Disobedience

3. 13th April 1919

4. Poona Pact

5. Abanindranath Tagore

TRUE OR FALSE

1. Depressed Classes Association was established by Ali brothers.

2. During the "Swadeshi Movement" in Bengal the flag designed was a Tricolour Flag.

3. The idea of Satyagraha emphasized on achieving independence through violence.

4. The resolution of Purna Swaraj was adopted at Lahore Session of 1929.

5. The Civil Disobedience Movement did not witness women participation.

Solutions

1. False

2. True

3. False

4. True

5. False

The Making of a Global World

Summary

The Pre modern World and the Nineteenth Century (Global Economy and Colonialism)

- Globalisation is a process of integration by sharing ideas, technology, culture and tradition.
- Trade with other countries and migration enabled the Globalisation.
- Money, skills, goods, ideas travelled a long distance with religious person, traders.
- We had some specific routes for trade, which enabled the access of knowledge, food products, skill and germs from one place to another. These routes were known as silk routes.
- Silk routes connects the Asia, Europe and Northern Africa.
- Food materials travelled with the traders and food produced in many part of the world, like the spaghetti of Italy was travelled from china. In china it was noodles.
- Some food materials like soya, ground nuts, potatoes, chillies, tomatoes travelled in Europe and Asia after discovery of America.
- European conquest American colonies with the help of small pox.

Nineteenth Century (Global Economy and Colonialism)

- In 19th century the society improved rapidly due to intermingle of, cultural, social and technological factors.
- Three types of movements took place in the economical context of the world in 19th century.
- First one was the hike in the trade of cloths and wheat. Second was the migration of people in search of job and third was the investment of money at small or large scale.

Global Economy

- In Britain the population was increasing but not the land. The government banned the import of corn to satisfy the landed group.
- Industrialist and urban dwellers were unhappy with the high food price and mounted pressure to lift the banned from corn laws.
- Consumption of food material increased but not the price. British farmers were not able to compete with markets they started to migrate.
- The purchasing power of peoples in England increased by faster industrial growth, Now the Eastern Europe, Australia, America started to cultivate to meet the demands of Britain.
- Agricultural regions needed to connect with ports or other centre for trade therefore infrastructural development took place like setup of Railways and making of Harbours.
- All development work and agriculture needed work force, that was fulfilled by the migrated labours of America and Australia
- Britishers developed canal to irrigate the land for growing cotton, to meet the demands of industries.

- The important inventions also paced the globalization of economies,especially means of transportation made easier to trade of perishable goods like meat. Now the meat is transported from America, Australia to Europe.

Colonialism

- The freedom of some countries was captured by developed ones, to meet the demands. It was the dark face of globalization.

- European powers to capture the geographical part to meet the demands they divided Africa for their means.

- In 1885 the European powers met in Berlin to divide Africa legally.

- The Belgium and Germany, Britain and France captured the geographical areas and became colonial powers.

- The colonies were used to fulfil the need of masters. The social economical exploitation placed the colonies in miserable conditions.

The Inter War and Post War Economy

- The first world war was continued more than four year, it was the industrial war.

- Technology, weapons, guns were used at large scale in this war. A millions of soldiers were recruited. 20 million soldiers injured.

- To meet the demands of war the industries were re-structured. Women started to do the work of men as men were involved in war.

- Britain took high amount of money from US to meet his war expenses.

- War changed the status of US from borrower to lender.

- The post war economy changed the economical scenario of the world.

- The condition of Britain was deplorable after the war. It was very tough to gain its status again.

- Britain lost his dominance in Indian market and was not able to compete with Japan.

- During war the production was increased due to high demand but after war production went down and unemployment increased.

- End of war created unemployment at large scale in Britain.

- After the war the production of wheat increased in Canada, Australia and America while decreased in Eastern Europe. The condition of agricultural economies were worsened after the war.

- After the war price of grains were fallen, incomes became declined.

- After war the economy of US went up due to mass production.

- Henry Ford, owner of Ford cars, used conveyer belt for mass production which was later followed by Europe.

- After the war the great depression was faced by many countries like US, India.

- After the world war, over production, fall of price of products, collapse of banks in US, fall in trade were the major reason of the Great Depression

Points to know

Biological war – a war in which germs, bacteria or other microorganism is used to defeat the enemy.

Dissenter – who is not going to accept the beliefs and practices, prevailing in society.

Indentured labour – a labour, bonded with a contract to work for employer for a frame time after that he can return his home. They termed as Girmitiya majdoor.

Exchange rate – for the purpose of international trade, the value of money is fix, to change it from other, national currencies.

Silk routes – a route which connected the Asia to its various regions also from Europe and Africa.

El Dorado – city of Gold

Important Personalities

Shikaripuri shroffs and Nattukottai Chettiars – were made a group of bankers to provide economical assistance in trade and agriculture.

Henery ford – owner of ford motors, who started the use of conveyer belt for production.

Important Dates

1890 – US become colonial power

1890 – Cattle plague and Rinderpest in Africa.

1800 – Indian cotton decline at 15%

1929 – The great depression

1928-34 – Price of wheat fall by 50 %

1944 – Bretton wood conference took place

PREVIOUS YEARS'
EXAMINATION QUESTIONS

▷ 1 Mark Questions

1. People's livelihoods and local economy of which one of the following was badly affected by the disease named 'Rinderpest'?

   (*a*) Asia

   (*b*) Europe

   (*c*) Africa

   (*d*) South America

   [TERM 1, 2011]

2. Which one of the following powerful weapons was used by the Spanish conquerors to colonise America during the mid seventeenth century?

   (*a*) Conventional Military Weapons

   (*b*) Modern Military Weapons

   (*c*) Biological Weapons (Germs of small pox)

   (*d*) Nuclear Weapons

   [TERM 1, 2011]

3. From where did most of the Indian Indentured Workers come from?

   [TERM 1, 2015]

4. Why did big European powers meet in Berlin in 1885?

   [DELHI 2018]

▷ 3 Mark Questions

5. Give three examples to show that the world changed with the discovery of new sea routes to America.

   [TERM 1, 2011]

6. What were Corn Laws? Why were these laws abolished? What were its results?

   [TERM 1, 2012]

7. Why did MNCs began to shift their production centres to Asian countries? What were its effects?

   [TERM 1, 2013]

8. Explain the impact of the First World War on the British economy.

   [TERM 1, 2014]

9. Explain the three types of "flows" within the international economic exchanges.

   [TERM 1, 2014]

10. Explain any three effects of the Great Depression of 1929 in the United States.

    [TERM 1, 2015]

11. "19th century indenture had been described as a new system of slavery". Explain the statement briefly.

    [TERM 1, 2015]

12. State three reasons why did Europeans flee to America in 19th century.

    [TERM 1, 2016]

13. Describe the impact of 'Rinderpest' on people's livelihoods and local economy in Africa in the 1890s.

    [DELHI 2018]

▷ 4 Mark Questions

14. Describe the causes of Great Depression.

    [TERM 1, 2011]

15. Explain any four features of primitive subsistence agriculture in India.

    [TERM 1, 2011]

▷ 5 Mark Questions

16. What attracted the Europeans to Africa? Mention any three methods used to recruit and retain the African laborers.

    [TERM 1, 2014]

17. Describe the effects of the Great Depression on the US.

    [TERM 1, 2012]

⚲ Solutions______________

1. (*c*) Africa [1]

2. (*c*) Biological Weapons (Germs of small pox) [1]

3. Most of the Indian Indentured Workers came from the regions of eastern Uttar Pradesh, Bihar, Central India and the dry districts of Tamilnadu. [1]

4. European powers met in Berlin in 1885 to decide the sharing of Africa among them. [1]

5. The world changed in the following ways with the discovery of new sea routes to America:

   (*i*) Many common foods were introduced to Europe from America e.g. Soya, Tomatoes, Potatoes, Maize, etc. Potato became the food for poor people. They began to eat better and live longer in England. [1]

   (*ii*) Europe started using Silver, a precious metal to enhance its wealth and finance its trade. These silver mines are located in present day Peru. [1]

   (*iii*) Europe started slave trades. Slaves were captured by European traders and taken to America. These slaves worked on plantations. Europe soon became the centre of the world trade. [1]

6. The restrictions of tariff and trade on the import of corn were Corn Laws. These were imposed between 1815 and 1846 by the British government in Great Britain. [1]

Because of the unhappiness of the industrialists and urban dweller due to hike in food prices, these laws were terminated as the price of grains was very high. [1]

The abolition of the Corn Laws resulted in free trade in Britain. Food could be imported into Britain at cheaper rates as a result, since agriculture was not able to compete with imports. This resulted in migration of farmers to urban areas in search of employment. [1]

7. MNCs began to shift their production centres to Asian countries because of the following reasons:

(i) Cheap labor and low wages. [1]

(ii) Availability of raw materials and a large market. [1]

It simulated world trade and also flow of capital. Countries like India, China and Brazil underwent rapid economic transformation. It generated employment opportunities and introduced competition in the domestics markets. [1]

8. The First World War had a very bad impact on the British economy. Some of the effects are as follows:

(i) 15-25% part of their stockpiled wealth was spent on the war, and after the war they had to suffer massive debts, especially from US. [1]

(ii) Britain had many buyers before the war. But after the war, it realized that its many buyers did not need to buy goods from Britain anymore as they had set up their own industries. It was because it could not provide goods for its foreign buyers during the war. [1]

(iii) The farmers also suffered because of the war as they had to produce more crops in the period of war but when the war ended, they had excess stock of the crops. As a result of it, prices declined and farmers had to face a great loses. [1]

(iv) In the period of war, many industries failed to modernize.

9. The three flows within the international economic exchanges were flow of trade, flow of labour and flow of capital.

(i) Flow of Trade: The trade in goods like cotton, wheat etc. is referred as the flow of trade.

In the beginning, the weavers of India used to produce cotton cloth and export it to European countries. [1]

(ii) Flow of Labour: In order to find the employment, people used to migrate and this migration is referred to as flow of labour. Many Indians migrated from India to Africa and other countries in search of employment in the 19th century. [1]

(iii) Flow of Capital: The movement of capital for long or short term investments over long distances is referred as the flow of capital. [1]

10. (i) The great depression began around 1929 and lasted till the mid-1930s. During this period most parts of the world experienced disastrous declines in production, employment, incomes and trade. [1]

(ii) The depression directly affected the Indian trade. India's exports and imports nearly cut down by 50% between 1928 and 1934. [1]

(iii) As international prices crashed, prices in India also got imported.

(iv) Peasants and farmers suffered more than urban residents. They got trapped in indebtedness. [1]

(v) The jute producers of Bengal were hard hit by this depression.

(vi) The price of raw jute fell by 60 % and as a result, the jute growers fell deeper and deeper in debt.

11. (i) Agents attracted the poor people by giving incorrect facts about the nature of work, place of work, living and working conditions, means of travel, etc. The living and working conditions were harsh for the people. [1]

(ii) Less willing workers were at time forcibly kidnapped by the agents. Workers had few legal rights. [1]

(iii) On arrival at the plantations, when laborers found conditions to be different, many of them escaped into the wilds. If they were caught, they were severely punished. [1]

12. (i) Economic crisis, increased poverty and hunger compelled people to leave Europe. [1]

(ii) Cities were crowded and deadly diseases were widespread. [1]

(iii) Religious conflicts were common and religious dissenters were persecuted. [1]

13. Impact of Rinderpest on Africa-

    (*i*) 90% of cattle were killed by Rinderpest. [1]

    (*ii*) Livelihood was destroyed due to loss of cattle. [1]

    (*iii*) People were forced into labour market. [1]

    (*iv*) European colonizers were able to conquer and subdue Africa when they got control over the cattle resources.

14. The causes of Great Depression are as follows:

    (*i*) There was an immense industrial expansion due to the increased demand of goods supplied to the army, during the period of the First World War. After the war, the demand for these goods suddenly dropped and so, there was no demand in many industries. There was also a large fall in the agricultural prices due to reduced demand. [1]

    (*ii*) In the mid-1920s, many countries financed their investments through loans from the USA. While it was often very easy to raise loans in the USA during the boom period, lenders in the USA panicked at the first sign of trouble. Countries that depended crucially on US loans, now faced an acute crisis. [1]

    (*iii*) Agricultural over production was another major factor responsible for the depression. This was made worse by falling agricultural prices. As prices slumped and agricultural incomes declined, the farmers tried to increase the production and bring a larger volume of produce to the market to maintain their overall income. This worsened the situation by pushing down the prices of farm produce further. [1]

    (*iv*) Large-scale unemployment: Farmers could not sell their harvests and businesses collapsed. As a result, large scale unemployment occurred. [1]

15. The following points explain the attributes of primitive subsistence agriculture in India:

    (*i*) This type of farming is performed on small land areas. The primitive tools such as hoe, Dao and digging sticks are used with the help of family/community. [1]

    (*ii*) In primitive subsistence agriculture, land availability per hectare is very low. [1]

    (*iii*) It is dependent upon the natural conditions such as monsoon, natural soil fertility and also other suitable environmental conditions, which are responsible for the growth of the crops. [1]

    (*iv*) This type of agriculture is done for self-consumption by the farmers. [1]

16. The Europeans got attracted to Africa due to the following reasons:

    (*i*) The Europeans were in search of the precious minerals like coal, silver and gold etc. [1]

    (*ii*) Africa had enormous resources of land. [1]

    (*iii*) They hoped to start mines and plantations in Africa. [1]

    The three methods used to recruit and retain the African laborers were:

    (*i*) Due to the imposition of heavy taxes by The Colonial government, the African laborers were forced to work for wages on plantations and mines. [1]

    (*ii*) The peasants were also displaced from the land because of the change in the Inheritance laws. According to this law, only one family member could inherit the land and as a result of it, others were forced to work in the labour market. [1]

    (*iii*) Minors were not allowed to move out and they were enclosed at the workplace.

17. The great depression was an economic crisis that started in 1929 and ended in mid 1930s. The effect of the Great Depression on the US was:

    (*i*) US experienced decline in production, demand, employment, trade and incomes. [1]

    (*ii*) Mass migration was experienced in major cities of USA and there was increase in crime rate, alcoholism and suicide. [1]

    (*iii*) Because of unemployment workers opted theft for food and survival and alcohol and suicide to escape from despair. [1]

    (*iv*) There was a huge decrease of enrolment in education sector and demographic system was also affected. Birth rate and divorce rate dropped and marriages were delayed. [1]

    (*v*) Banking system in US collapsed and banks ran out of money. [1]

MULTIPLE CHOICE QUESTIONS

1. The laws allowing the British Government to restrict the import of corn were known as:

   (*a*) Corn Laws

   (*b*) Indentured labour

   (*c*) Cowrie

   (*d*) Dissenter

2. Why did the wheat price fall down by 50 per cent between 1928 and 1934?

   (*a*) Droughts

   (*b*) Due to less production

   (*c*) Due to floods

   (*d*) Due to the Great Depression

3. The network of routes connecting Asia with Europe and Northern Africa is called as......?

   (*a*) Sea Route   (*b*) Silk Route

   (*c*) Panama Islands   (*d*) Atlantic Drift

4. Which of these was a well-known Pioneer of mass production?

   (*a*) Ratan Tata   (*b*) Wright Brothers

   (*c*) Henry Ford   (*d*) Albert Einstein

5. What does G-77 stands for?

   (*a*) It refers to the seventy seven developing countries that did not benefit from the fast growth western economies experienced in 1950s and 1960s.

   (*b*) It refers to the seventy seven developed countries

   (*c*) It refers to a group of 77 intellectual people

   (*d*) Both (*a*) and (*c*)

Answer Keys

1. (*a*)   2. (*d*)   3. (*b*)   4. (*c*)   5. (*a*)

FILL IN THE BLANKS

1. Most Indian indentured workers came from ____________________.

2. ____________ is referred to as the Bretton Woods twins.

3. In 1890, a fast spreading disease of ________ had a terrifying impact on people's livelihoods in Africa.

4. The Great Depression occurred in the year________.

5. ______________ is an imaginary city of gold situated in South America

Solutions

1. Eastern Uttar Pradesh

2. The International Monetary Fund (IME) and the World Bank

3. Rinderpest

4. 1929

5. El Dorado

TRUE OR FALSE

1. Indian exports and imports nearly halved between1928-1934.

2. Europeans were attracted to Africa due to availability of milk.

3. When the disease destroyed the potato crop, Ireland's, poor peasants died of starvation.

4. Christopher Columbus discovered the African continent

5. The United Nations Monetary and Financial Conference held at San Francisco in 1944.

Solutions

1. True

2. False

3. True

4. False

5. False

The Age of Industrialization

Summary

Industrialization in India

- Silk and finer varieties of cotton of India had a larger demand in international market before the uses of machines.

- Goods were taken from Punjab by Persian and Armenian trader, had sent in Afghanistan and central Asia.

- There was a trade link between many countries through Hooghly port, Surat port, and financing production importing goods was done by various Indian merchants, capitalist and bankers.

- Network of trade relating with various countries was controlled by the Indians merchant and traders.

- But taking grants and monopoly from local courts and kings the European countries, slowly controlled over the trade. This led the declination of Indian traders and bankers.

- European traders replaced the ports from Surat and Hooghly to Calcutta and Bombay.

- The entrance of east India company changed the manual weaving industries, economic assistance started to provide as a loan to weavers to manufacture cloths and entire manufacturing activity was supervised by Gomasthas.

- The situation led the migration of weavers as they were not able to survive.

- The development of cotton industries, led the britishers to sell cotton in Indian market, the Indian weavers could not compete with the machine products of England.

- There was a huge decline in the cotton industries of due to European cotton.

Factories in India

- In Bombay the first cotton mill was set up in 1854.

- In Bengal first jute mill was set up in 1855, the eligin mill was started in Kanpur and first spinning and weaving mills were setup in Madras.

- Some of Indian traders were involved in trade with china and earned huge profit.

- In Bengal the Dwarakanath Tagore setup six joint stock company to trade with china.

- In Bombay Dinshaw petit and Jamset ji tata established huge business empire in India and were involved in trade with China.

- Hukumchand and G.D birla also setup the industries in India after making huge profit from trade with China.

- The merchant, bankers and trader who were involved in carrying goods and supply within countries also setup industries in India after earning huge profit.

- The setup of industries changed the social scenario as the workers were employed by the jobbers at large scale.

Industrialization in Britain

- England had a huge production of products before the age of machine that age is termed as proto industrialisation in England.

- Merchants started to connect with workers in village and offered economical assistance for production of goods

- Due to increase in world trade, merchants were not able to produce goods with urban crafts therefore they moved towards village and offered work to poor peasants.

- By using the working capacities of all family the peasants were able to fulfil the demands of merchants and by manufacturing goods they raised their income.

- A network was developed by merchants before the age of machines strengthened the relationship between town and villages.

- By 1730, factories came up in England after that a number of factories were setup by the late eighteenth centuries.

- Cotton was the symbol of new age ,the increase of the production changed the status of England

- A series of inventions took place for the development of cotton industries.

- With the help of technology production process like carding, twisting, spinning and rolling, were improved. The Richard Arkwright made a cotton mill.

- With high production rate factories became lifeline of England. It was the leading sector of England.

- The demand of iron and steel went up after the development of Railway.

- A large part production was taking place outside the factories, it was not possible to displace traditional industries.

- The worker of mid nineteenth century was a manual worker not the machine operator.

- The demand for labour in industries was seasonal, in season based industries there was a manual (hand working) labour. Industries of England had a wide range of products made by hand.

- The upper class was the main user of hand made products therefore the products of machine was exported in colonies.

- The machine was used in production where the availability of labours was less.

- The job opportunities was affected by the large number of availability of labours,

Points to know

Stapler – a person who sorts wool according to its fibres.

Carding – a process of preparing Fibres.

Bourgeoise – the upper middle class.

Gomastha – a agent or paid servant under the britishers to play a role of middle man between weavers and merchants.

Trade guilds – association of producers.

Important Personalities

Richard Arkwright – created cotton mill.

James Watt – improved the steam engine.

Mathew Bolten – manufactured the new model of steam engines.

Jamest Ji Tata – Founder of TATA.

Important Dates

1854 - in India the First cotton mill was set up

1730 - in England the Earliest factory was set up

1760 - 2.5 millions pounds of raw materials was imported by Britain

1840 - Expansion of cotton in England

1860 - Expansion of railway in England

1764 - Spinning Jenny was Invented.

1750 - breaking down of Indian merchant network

1855 - in Bengal First Jute mill was established

1733 - Flying shuttle invented

1779 - Invention of mules

PREVIOUS YEARS'
EXAMINATION QUESTIONS

▶ **1 Mark Questions**

1. Which of the following mechanical devices was used for weaving with ropes and pullies, which helped to weave wide pieces of cloth?
   (*a*) Handloom   (*b*) Power loom
   (*c*) Fly shuttle   (*d*) Spinning Jenny
   [TERM 1, 2011]

2. Which of the following were the Pre-Colonial ports of India?
   (*a*) Surat and Masulipatam
   (*b*) Madras and Hoogly
   (*c*) Madras and Bombay
   (*d*) Bombay and Hoogly
   [TERM 1, 2011]

3. Where was the first Indian Jute Mill set up?
   [TERM 1, 2013]

4. In which year did the first cotton mill in Bombay(Mumbai) come up?
   [TERM 1, 2015]

5. Who adopted the assembly line production of cars?
   [TERM 1, 2016]

6. Which was the first country to undergo industrial revolution?
   [TERM 1, 2016]

7. Between which place the first section of the underground railway in the world was opened?
   [TERM 1, 2016]

8. Why did merchants from towns in Europe begin to move to countryside in seventeenth and eighteenth centuries?
   [DELHI 2018]

▶ **3 Mark Questions**

9. What technique of advertisement did Manchester industrialists use to entice the Indian consumers?
   [TERM 1, 2011]

10. Why were Jobbers employed by Indian industrialists?
    [TERM 1, 2012, 2015]

11. Why did women workers in Britain attack the Spinning Jenny? Give any reasons.
    [TERM 1, 2013]

12. Describe the condition of the workers in nineteenth century in England?
    [TERM 1, 2014]

13. What were guilds? How did they make it difficult for new merchants to set business in towns of England? Explain.
    [TERM 1, 2014]

14. Describe the contributions of Dwarakanath Tagore as an entrepreneur of Bengal.
    [TERM 1, 2015]

15. What is meant by "Trade Surplus"? Why did Britain have a trade surplus with India?
    [TERM 1, 2016]

16. "Although wages increased somewhat in the nineteenth century yet they could not improve the welfare of the workers," How do you agree with this statement? Explain any three points?
    [TERM 1, 2016]

17. "The old ports of Surat and Hoogly declined by the end of the 18th century". Why? Explain any three reasons.
    [TERM 1, 2016]

18. Describe any three major problems faced by Indian cotton weavers in nineteenth century.
    [DELHI 2018]

▶ **4 Mark Questions**

19. How did the East India Company procure regular supplies of cotton and silk textiles from Indian weavers?
    [TERM 1, 2011]

▶ **5 Mark Questions**

20. What problems did the cotton weavers face in India?
    [TERM 1, 2012]

21. 'Bombay was a Prime city of India." Justify by giving examples.
    [TERM 1, 2012]

22. "The modern Industrialization could not marginalize the traditional industries in England." Justify the statement with any four suitable arguments.
    [TERM 1, 2013]

23. Explain the process of industrialization in Britain during the nineteenth century.
    [TERM 1, 2014]

24. "In the eighteenth century Europe, the peasants and artisans in the countryside readily agreed to work for the merchants." Explain any three reasons. [TERM 1, 2015]

Solutions

1. (c) Fly shuttle [1]

2. (a) Surat and Masulipatam [1]

3. The first jute mill was set up at Rishra, on the River Hooghly near Calcutta. [1]

4. In 1854, "The Bombay Spinning Mill", was the first cotton mill in Bombay. [1]

5. Henry Ford installed the first moving assembly line for the mass production of an entire automobile. [1]

6. Britain was the first country to undergo industrial revolution. [1]

7. On 10th January 1863, the first section of the underground railway in the world was opened between Paddington and Farrington Street in London. [1]

8. Merchants began to move to countryside in the 17th & 18th centuries because

   (i) They could not expand production within towns. [0.5]

   (ii) The trade guilds restricted the entry of new people into the trade in towns. [0.5]

9. Following techniques were used by Manchester industrialists to entice the Indian consumers:

   (i) These industrialists took advantage of people's religious values. The products were produced with pictures of god and goddess printed on it. This was done to attract people towards their products. [1]

   (ii) As these goods were machine made, they sold it at cheap rates that attracted Indian consumer because they were purchasing handmade goods at very high prices. [1]

   (iii) They spent large amount of money in the advertisement. There were posters of their products everywhere. [1]

10. Jobbers were employed by Indian industrialists:

   (i) To get new recruits as they were very often an old and trusted worker. As the mills multiplied, the demand of workers went up. [1]

   (ii) They got jobs for people and helped them settle in cities and in crisis. [1]

   (iii) They became powerful and started demanding money and gifts for their favours and also started controlling the lives of the workers. [1]

11. The women workers in Britain attacked the Spinning Jenny because:

   (i) The spinning wheel was able to spin many spindles with one wheel. This led to decrease in employment of women for spinning. [1]

   (ii) The women opposed the new technology because of the fear of unemployment. [1]

12. In the mid-nineteenth century, the workers in England were wrong in very bad conditions. However after 1840, their condition got better due to urbanization. But they had to suffer a lot till 1840. It can be understood as follows:

   (i) The employment of the workers was dependent on their social networks. The workers who had good connections in the factories or had friends and relatives there could get work easily. So it was difficult for those who had no connections in the factories. [1]

   (ii) The employment was seasonal. The workers had to stay unemployed once the busy period was over. Most of the workers wanted to have odd jobs but it was quite difficult to find at that time. [1]

   (iii) The workers had a fear of unemployment due to the introduction of new technology. [1]

   (iv) In the early nineteenth century, the wages rate was increased somehow but the prices were also increased and as a result, that increment got nullified.

13. The associations of merchants or artisans who controlled their craft practices and trade in any distinct city were known as guilds. The rulers granted them monopoly rights to produce and trade in some particular products so they were very powerful. They used to train the people themselves and regulated the competition. The entry of new people in the trade was also restricted by them. Therefore new merchants faced difficulty in setting up business in the towns of England. [1 + 1 + 1]

14. (*i*) Dwarakanath Tagore was in favour of the fact that by westernization and industrialization, India would develop. [1]

(*ii*) He made huge investments in banking, shipping, mining, plantations and in insurance. [1]

(*iii*) Dwarakanath Tagore made industrial investments and set up six Joint Stock Companies between 1830s and 1840s. He also made a fortune in China. [1]

15. When the value of exports is higher than the value of imports, then this difference is called the trade surplus. [1]

Britain had a trade surplus with India because of:

(*i*) British colonialism in India and their economic policies. [1]

(*ii*) The higher value of British exports to India than the Indian exports to Britain. [1]

Britain used this trade surplus to balance their trade deficits. Britain's trade surplus also helped it to pay private remittance back to Britain by British officials and traders, interest payment of India's external debt and business of British officials in India.

16. (*i*) The prices of different commodities rose sharply during the prolonged Napoleonic war, and even with the increased in wages the workers could only buy fewer things. [1]

(*ii*) The workers did not get employment everyday and their average daily income was determined by the number of days they worked. [1]

(*iii*) In 1830s, the proportion of unemployment went up to between 35 and 75 per cent in different regions. [1]

17. The old ports of Surat and Hoogly declined by the end of the 18th century because:

(*i*) The European companies slowly gained power, by first taking a huge amount of concessions from the local courts and then having the monopoly on the trade rights. [1]

(*ii*) Exports from these ports started to fall suddenly. The credit that was given earlier began to become less and the local bankers gradually started to go bankrupt. [1]

(*iii*) In the last years of the 17th century, the gross value of trade that passed through Surat decreased to Rs.16 million. Thre was a shift in European companies towards Bombay and Calcutta, which caused the decline of old ports. [1]

18. Major problems faced by the Indian cotton weavers-

(*i*) Their export market collapsed. [0.5]

(*ii*) The local market shrunk and was glutted with Manchester products . [0.5]

(*iii*) There was increase in price of raw cotton. [0.5]

(*iv*) There was shortage of cotton. [0.5]

(*v*) It was difficult for weavers to compete with the imported machine made cheaper cotton products. [0.5]

(*vi*) Factories in India also began making cheaper machine made goods with which our weavers could not compete. [0.5]

19. The following are the various steps adopted by the East India Company to ensure regular supplies of cotton and silk textiles.

(*i*) They established political power to assert monopoly right to trade. [1]

(*ii*) They developed a system of 'managing and control' to eliminate any competition, control cost and ensure regular supply of cotton and silk goods. [1]

(*iii*) They eliminated the existing traders as well as the broker that had any link with cloth and made direct links with the weaver. [1]

(*iv*) They appointed paid servants and called them 'gomasthas' in order to supervise weavers, examine the quality of the cloth and collect supplies. [1]

(*v*) Weavers were not allowed to contact other buyers. Weavers were given advances and were offered loans to buy raw material. Those who took advance or loan could not contact any other trader.

(*vi*) The weavers had to sell at a price dictated by the Company. By giving loan the Company tied the weavers with them.

20. Problems faced by cotton weaver in India were as follows:

 (*i*) There was long decline in export of textile in India. [1]

 (*ii*) There was not sufficient supply of good quality raw cotton. [1]

 (*iii*) Cheap machine made cotton goods was imported and the weavers were not able to easily compete with that. [1]

 (*iv*) Since there was not sufficient supply of good quality raw cotton, so weavers had to buy raw cotton at a very high price. [1]

 (*v*) By the end of 19th century textile factories were set up in India flooding the market with machine made goods, which made situation difficult for the weavers to survive. [1]

21. 'Bombay was a Prime city of India' because of the following reasons:

 (*i*) In the 17th century Bombay was under Portuguese control and it was a group of seven islands. [1]

 (*ii*) Control of Bombay was passed into the hands of British after the marriage of Portuguese princess with King of Britain. [1]

 (*iii*) The East India Company quickly shifted its principal western port from Surat to Bombay. [1]

 (*iv*) By the beginning of 19th century, Bombay was functioning as a port through which huge quantities of raw material such as cotton and opium would pass. [1]

 (*v*) Bombay slowly became one of the most important administrative centre of Western India. [1]

 (*vi*) By the end of 19th century, Bombay becomes a major industrial centre.

22. The modern industrialization could not marginalize the traditional industry in England because:-

 (*i*) Less than 20% of total workforce was employed in technologically advanced industrial sectors even at the end of the 19th Century. Textiles was a dynamic sector but a large portion of the output was produced within domestic units. [1 + 1]

 (*ii*) Small and ordinary innovations were the basis of growth in many non-mechanized sectors such as construction, pottery, glass work, tanning, furniture making, food-processing and making of tools. [1]

 (*iii*) Technological changes occurred slowly. New technology was expensive and the merchants and industrialists were cautious about using it. [1]

 (*iv*) The machines often broke down and their repair was costly. [1]

23. The process of industrialization in Britain during the 19th century was as follows:

 (*i*) The process of industrialization began with the installment of the major industries like cotton and metal. After that the iron and steel industries were also established and these industries started increasing rapidly as the railways were expanded in England and its colonies. So Britain started exporting steel and iron and their cost was double of the cost of cotton export. [1]

 (*ii*) The conventional industries could not easily be replaced by the new technologies. The workforce employed in the advanced industries was very low. Though the textile industry was a major one, still most of the output was produced in the domestic units. [1]

 (*iii*) In some of the non-mechanized sectors like building, glass work, food processing, pottery, furniture making etc. small inventions like steam powered cotton industries built the base of the growth. [1]

 (*iv*) The efficiency of the production process was increased by the new inventions. The cotton mill was established by Richard Arkwright. [1]

The rate of execution of the technology was very low. New machineries were very costly so they could not spread rapidly. Also the repairing of the machines was expensive if they broke down. They were not found as effective as they were supposed to be. [1]

24. **In the eighteenth century Europe, the peasants and artisans in the countryside readily agreed to work for the merchants due to the following reasons:** [1]

    (*i*) **The poor peasants were dependent on an open field and common lands for their firewood, vegetables, straws and hay which were disappearing.** [1]

    (*ii*) **Peasants were not able to provide work for all the members of the family due to tiny owned plots which are not sufficient for all of them.** [1]

    (*iii*) **They were offered advances by merchants to produce goods for them. With this, the peasants could cultivate their small lands and could stay in the countryside.** [1]

    (*iv*) **Peasants and artisans could supplement their agricultural income with that of the income from the merchants' work.** [1]

MULTIPLE CHOICE QUESTIONS

1. Which machine was invented by James Hargreaves in 1764?
   (*a*) Spinning Jenny
   (*b*) Fully automatic machine
   (*c*) Steam Iron
   (*d*) Car polishing

2. Steam Engine was patented by?
   (*a*) Henry Ford   (*b*) Richard Arkwright
   (*c*) James Watt   (*d*) James Hargreaves

3. The first cotton mill in India was set up at?
   (*a*) Madras   (*b*) Gujarat
   (*c*) Punjab   (*d*) Bombay

4. A person employed by the industrialists to get new recruits for the mills was called as….
   (*a*) Dyer   (*b*) Jobber
   (*c*) Sepoy   (*d*) Vagrant

5. Whom did the British government appoint to supervise weavers collect supplies and to examine the quality of cloth?
   (*a*) Entrepreneur   (*b*) Sepoy
   (*c*) Policeman   (*d*) Gomastha

Answer Keys

   1. (*a*)   2. (*c*)   3. (*d*)   4. (*b*)   5. (*d*)

FILL IN THE BLANKS

1. _____________, an Indian port lost its importance during colonial rule

2. New technology like_______________________ helped in increased the handloom cloth production in the early 20th century.

3. The early phase of industrialisation was known as________________.

4. The first spinning and weaving mill set up in 1874 at _______________.

5. ____________ produced a music book in 1900.

Solutions

1. Surat
2. looms with fly shuttle
3. proto-industrialisation
4. Madras
5. E.T. Paull

TRUE OR FALSE

1. Industrialisation gave rise to imperialism.
2. The workers in England were overwhelmed with the coming up of machines and new technology.
3. Guild was an association of Indian workers employed by the East India Company.
4. The nationalists spread the message of Swadeshi through advertisements.
5. Advertisements like images of gods and goddesses frequently appeared on the labels of the cloth.

Solutions

1. True
2. False
3. False
4. True
5. True

Unit II : Geography

Minerals and Energy Resources

Summary

Minerals and mode of their occurrence.

- Naturally occurring homogenous substance with a definable internal structure.
- Minerals are usually found in Ores

Occurrence

- In the cracks of Igneous and metamorphic rocks
- The smaller occurrence is Lodes, and larger is Veins.
- Major metallic minerals like tin, copper, zinc and lead are obtained from loads and veins.
- In the bed or layers of sedimentary rocks, minerals like coal, gypsum, potash etc. are found.
- It is formed as a result of deposition, accumulation and concentration in horizontal strata.
- Another mode of formation involves the decomposition of surface rocks and the removal of soluble Constituents. Bauxite is formed by this way.
- In the placer deposits of sands minerals like gold, silver, tin and platinum are found.
- Common salt, magnesium and bromine are derived from the bed of oceans.

Ferrous and Non ferrous minerals and their conservation

- Three fourth of the total value of the production of metallic minerals
- India exports substantial quantities of ferrous minerals after his domestic use.

Ferrous

Orissa Jharkand Belt

- In Orissa high grade hematite ore is found in Badampahar mines in the Mayurbhanj and Kendujhar
- Gua and Noamundi of Jharkhand having haematite iron ore.
- Durg - Bastar - Chandrapur belt - Lies in chattisgarh and Maharashtra high grade hematitis are found in Bailadila range of hills in Chatisgarh.
- Bellavy Chitradurga - Chikmaglur - Tumkur Belt – In Karnataka has large reserves of iron ore. Kudermuch mines located in western Ghats of Karnataka and known to be one of the largest.
- Maharashtra - Goa Belt - Goa and Ratnagir district of Maharashtra have ample amount of ore. It is not of very high quality yet they are efficiently exploited.
- For manufacturing of steel and ferro-manganese alloy, manganese is obtained from Orrisa, the largest producer of it.

Non Ferrous

- **Copper** – The Balaghat mines of M.P produces 52 percent copper of total production. Khetri and Singhbhum of Jharkhand is important producer.
- It is used in electrical industries.

  Bauxite - Amarkantank plateau, Maikal hill and the region of Bilaspur–Katni have a ample amount of it.
- **Orrisa** produce 45 percent bauxite of total production. **Panchpatmali of koraput** is important producer.

Conservation

- Minerals required millions of years to be created and concentrated.
- The total workable minerals deposit is one percent of the earth crust, and are rapidly consuming.
- The geological processes of mineral formation are slower than the rate of replenishment.
- The present rate of consumption of finite and non renewable minerals is high.
- To extract the minerals from depth is become expensive.
- To ensure the availability of minerals resources in future, need to accept planned and sustainable use.
- Recycling of metals using scraps metal and other substitute are steps in conserving minerals resources for future.

Conventional sources of Energy

Coal-occurs mainly in west Bengal-Jharkhand, and Godavari, Mahanadi, Son, Wardha valley and Assam, Arunachal Pradesh.

Lignite is low grade iron ,major reserve are in Neyveli in Tamilnadu, is used for generating electricity.

- Bituminous coal is used in blast furnace for smelting iron and other commercial purpose.
- Anthracite is the highest quality of coal .

Petrolium - occurrence in India are associated with anticlines and fault traps in the rock formation of tertiary age.

- About 63 percent of India's is from Mumbai high and 16 percent from Assam.

- In Gujarat Ankeleshwar is the most important field. Digboi, Naharkatiya are the oil field of Assam.
- For synthetic textile, fertilizer and other chemical industries,it acts as a Nodal industry.

Natural gas - reserves found in the Krishna–Godavari basin, along the west coast of Mumbai high and Andaman-Nicobar islands.

The power and fertilizers industries are key users of natural gas.

Electricity - generated by fast flowing water of various multi- purpose river projects.

- electricity is also generated by the use of coal. There are over 310 thermal power plants in India.
- nuclear energy is also use for generation electricity. Uranium of Aravali and Jharkhand region is used to generate electricity.

Non conventional sources of Energy

Solar energy - the photovoltaic technology converts sunlight directly into electricity. It becomes very popular in remote and rural areas.

- Madhupur near Bhuj is the largest solar plant in India. it is used to sterilise milk cans.

Wind power - India rank as a wind super power in the world.

The largest wind farm cluster is located from Nagarcoli to Madurai of Tamilnadu.

Biogas - It is obtained by decomposition of organic materials as shrubs, farm waste, animal and human waste.

- The gobar gas plants provide twin benefits to the farmer in the form of energy and improved quality of manure.
- Tidal energy-oceanic tides is used to generate electricity.
- The gulf of kuchchh provides ideal condition for utilizing tidal energy. 900 MW tidal energy power plant is set up by National Hydro power .

Geo thermal energy – electricity is generated by the internal heat of the earth.

- Paravati valley near Manikarn in Himachal Pradesh and Puga valley of Ladakh is two experimental projects set up by the government to generate electricity.

Points to know

RAT HOLE MINING

In tribal area of north east India, especially in Meghalaya digging pits ranging from five to 100 m² into the ground to reach the coal seam by tribals to obtain coal.

PREVIOUS YEARS'
EXAMINATION QUESTIONS

▷ 1 Mark Questions

1. Which one of the following minerals is a fossil fuel?

   (*a*) Barium

   (*b*) Coal

   (*c*) Zircon

   (*d*) Uranium

   [TERM 2, 2011]

2. Orissa is the leading producer of which one of the following minerals?

   (*a*) Copper

   (*b*) Iron ore

   (*c*) Manganese ore

   (*d*) Mica

   [TERM 2, 2011]

3. Kodarma Gaya-Hazaribagh belt of Jharkhand is the leading producer of which one of the following minerals?

   (*a*) Copper

   (*b*) Bauxite

   (*c*) Iron-ore

   (*d*) Mica

   [TERM 2, 2012]

4. Which one of the following fuels is considered environment friendly?

   (*a*) Coal   (*b*) Petroleum

   (*c*) Natural gas   (*d*) Firewood

   [TERM 2, 2012]

5. How do minerals occur in sedimentary rocks?

   [TERM 2, 2015]

6. Why has aluminum metal great importance?

   [TERM 2, 2016]

▷ 3 Mark Questions

7. Make a distinction between hydroelectricity and thermal electricity stating the three points of distinction.

   [TERM 2, 2011]

8. Mention any three major iron-ore belts of India. Write any three characteristics of the southernmost iron-ore belt.

   [TERM 2, 2012]

9. Three features - A, B and C are marked in the given political outline map of India. Identify these features with the help of the following information and write their correct names on the lines marked in the map:

   (*a*) Iron-ore mine

   (*b*) Oil field

   (*c*) Terminal Station of NH. 7

   [TERM 2, 2012]

10. Differentiate between metallic and non-metallic minerals with examples.

    [TERM 2, 2013]

11. Which state is the largest producer of manganese in India? Mention any four uses of manganese.

    [TERM 2, 2013]

12. On the same political outline map of India, locate and label the following with appropriate symbols:

    (*i*) Narora – a nuclear power plant

    (*ii*) Rourkela – an iron and steel plant

    (*iii*) Kandla – a major sea port

    [TERM 2, 2014]

13. How can solar energy solve the energy problem to some extent in India? Give your opinion.

    [TERM 2, 2015]

14. (*i*) Two features A and B are marked on the given political outline map of India. Identify these features with the help of the following information and write their correct names on the lines marked in the map:

    A. Iron-ore mines

    B. Terminal Station of East-West Corridor

    (*ii*) On the same political outline map of India, locate and label the following:

    Vishakhapatnam – Software Technology Park   [TERM 2, 2015]

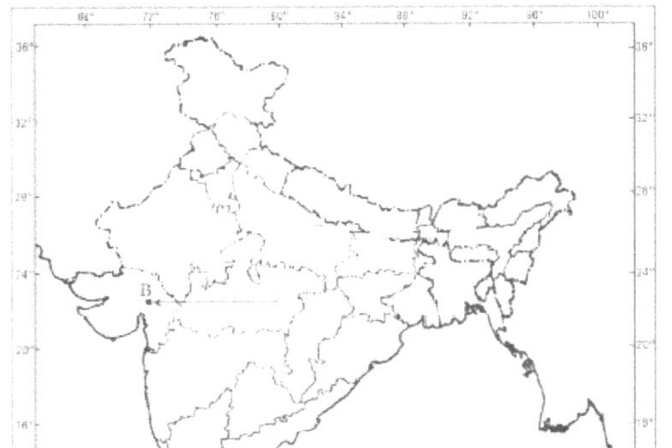

Outline Map of India (Political)

15. (a) In which state are Bailadila Iron-ore mines located ?

(b) Name the Western Terminal Station of East-West Corridor.

(c) Name the well-known Software Technology Park located in Karnataka State

[TERM 2, 2015]

16. 'Consumption of energy in all forms has been rising all over the country. There is an urgent need to develop a sustainable path of energy development and energy saving'. Suggest and explain any three measures to solve this burning problem.

[TERM 2, 2016]

17. On a given political map of India, locate and label the following with appropriate symbols:

A. Oil Field- Digboi

B. Iron and Steel Plant – Bhilai

C. Major Sea Port-Kochi.

Locate and label Rihand. On the same political map of India.

[TERM 2, 2014]

18. Describe any three characteristics of the Durg-Bastar-Chandrapur Iron-ore belt in India.

[TERM 2, 2017]

19. On the given political outline map of India locate and label the following features with appropriate symbols:

A. Naraura – Nuclear Power Plant

B. Tuticorin – Major Sea Port

C. Bhilai – Iron and Steel Plant

[TERM 2, 2017]

▶ 5 Mark Questions

20. Three features (a), (b), (c) are marked in the given political outline map of India. Identify these features with the help of the following information and write their correct names on the lines marked in the map:

(a) Coal mine

(b) Silk Industry

(c) International Airport

AND

Locate and label the following items on the same political outline map of India with appropriate symbols:

(i) Kanpur – Cotton Textile Industry

(ii) Bhadravati- Iron and Steel Plant

(iii) Kandla- Sea Port

[TERM 2, 2011]

21. Why is there a pressing need for using renewable energy sources in India? Explain any five reasons.

[TERM 2, 2014]

22. Which is the most abundantly available fossil fuel in India? Assess the importance of its different forms.

[TERM 2, 2015]

23. Why is it necessary to conserve mineral resources? Explain any four ways to conserve mineral resources.

[TERM 2, 2017]

🔑 Solutions

1. (b) Coal   [1]

2. (c) Manganese ore   [1]

3. (d) Mica   [1]

4. (c) Natural ga   [1]

5: Mineral occurs in beds or layers in sedimentary rocks.   [1]

6. Aluminum is an important metal because it combines the strength of metals such as iron, with extreme lightness and also with good conductivity and great malleability.   [1]

7. Electricity generated mainly in two ways can be recognized as Hydroelectricity and Thermal electricity.

Hydroelectricity is generated by hydropower that is water falling on turbines or fast flowing water. The sources are renewable that is inexhaustible.

It causes no pollution and is cheaper. Many multi-purpose projects are there in India, like Bhakra Nangal, Damodar Valley whereas Thermal Electricity is generated from petroleum (oil) or coal. Its source is non-renewable or exhaustible. Burning of coal and oil causes pollution and it is expensive. The number of Thermal Power Plants in India is more than 310.   [0.5 + 0.5 + 0.5 + 0.5 + 0.5 + 0.5]

8. The three major iron ore belts of India are: Orissa-Jharkhand belt, Durg-Bastar- Chandrapur belt lying in Chhattisgarh and Maharashtra and the Bellary-Chitradurga- Chikmaglur-Tumkur belt in Karnataka.   [1.5]

The three characteristics of the southernmost iron-ore belt i.e. Bellary-Chitradurga-Chikmaglur-Tumkur belt in Karnataka are:

(i) The Kudremukh mines are located in the Western Ghats of Karnataka and their entire produce is exported.

(ii) The Kudremukh deposits are one of the largest deposits of iron ore in the world.

(iii) Through a pipeline ore is transported as slurry to a port in Mangalore.   [1.5]

9.   [1 + 1]

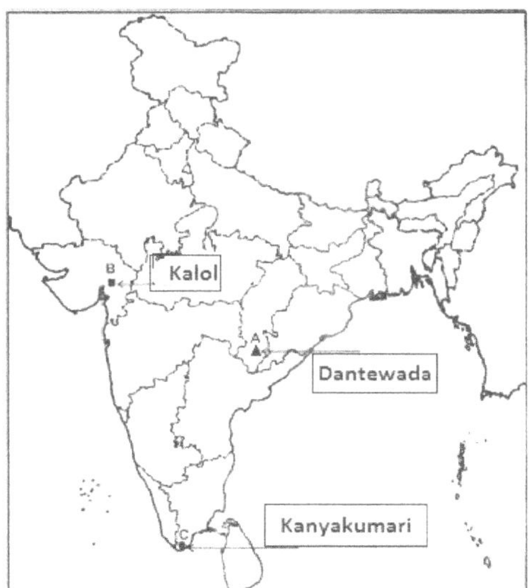

10.

Metallic Minerals	Non Metallic Minerals
They contain **metals in raw form**.	They **do not contain metals**. [1]
Metallic minerals have **higher boiling point and melting point**.	Non Metallic minerals have **lower boiling point and melting point**. [1]

Act as **good reducing agents**	Act as **good oxidizing agents** [1]
They are **lustrous, malleable and ductile**.	They are **brittle**.
Examples: Iron ore, Bauxite, Zinc and Lead	Examples: Limestone, Mica, Gypsum.

11. Odisha is the largest producer of manganese in India. Being a leading producer of manganese ore with a share of 22.62 % in India during 2010-11, it accounts for country's 44% of manganese ore.   [1]

Uses of manganese are:

(i) Mostly required in glass industry.   [1]

(ii) Helps in manufacturing bleaching powder in chemical industry.   [1]

(iii) Used to manufacture good quality steel.

(iv) Used for manufacturing alloys, pesticides and insecticides.

12.

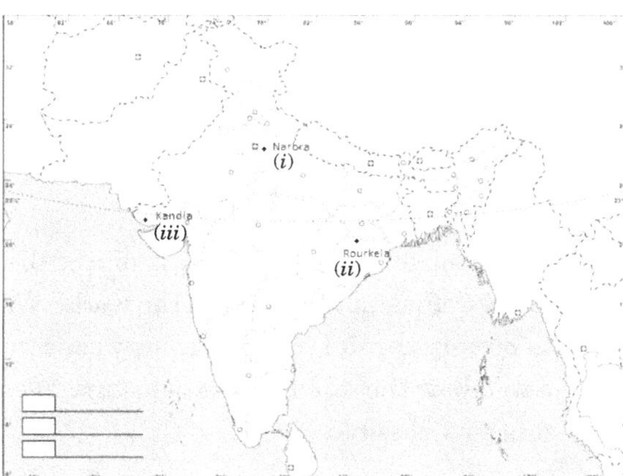

13. As India has enormous possibilities of tapping solar energy so it is known as a tropical country.   [1]

Sunlight can be converted into electricity directly using the Photovoltaic technology.   [1]

Solar energy is getting popular among rural areas. Some big solar power plants are being are established in different part of India which will minimize the dependence of rural households on firewood and dung cakes.   [1]

14. (i)

A. Iron-ore mines – Bellary   [1]

B. Terminal Station of East-West Corridor - Porbandar   [1] (*ii*) **Vishakhapatnam – Software Technology Park has been labeled in the map as follows:** [1]

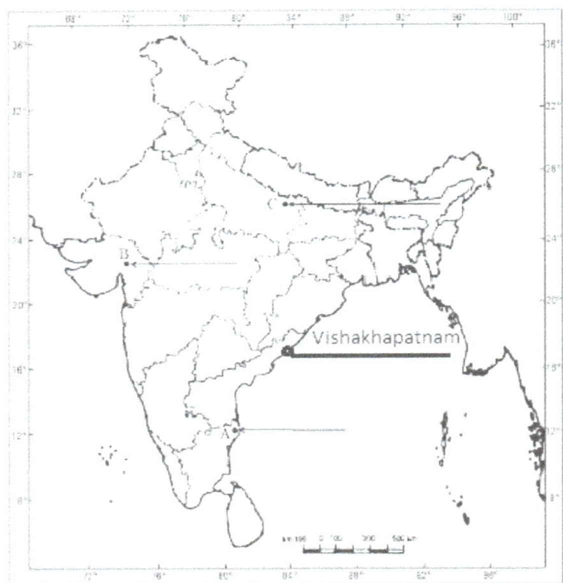

15. (*a*) **Chattisgarh** [1]

(*b*) **Porbandar** [1]

(*c*) **Electronic City** [1]

16. In present time, our country is one of the least energy efficient countries in the world. We need to be very careful towards energy consumption and follow the different ways to save energy as much as possible.

Below are a few measures to solve this burning problem:

(*i*) One should use public transport system instead of individual vehicles more often. [1]

(*ii*) Switching off the electricity when it is not in use, this should be in practice properly and due to this, we can incorporate a lot in energy conservation. [1]

(*iii*) Use more power saving devices and non-conventional sources of energy [1]

(*iv*) By encouraging young brains to innovate in alternative sources of energy.

17.

[1 + 1 + 1]

18. **The characteristics of the Durg-Bastar-Chandrapur Iron-ore belt are as follows:**

(*i*) **Durg-Bastar-Chandrapur Iron-ore belt lies in Chhattisgarh and Maharashtra.** [1]

(*ii*) **Hematite, a high-quality ore of iron is found in Bastar.** [1]

(*iii*) **14 high-quality hematite ore is found in the hills of this region.** [1]

19.   [1 + 1 + 1]

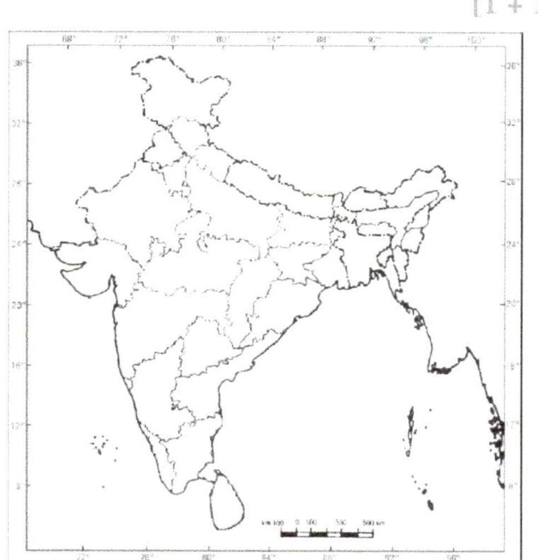

20.

(*a*) **Korba**   [1]

(*b*) **Murshidabad**   [1]

(*c*) **Chennai**   [1]

AND

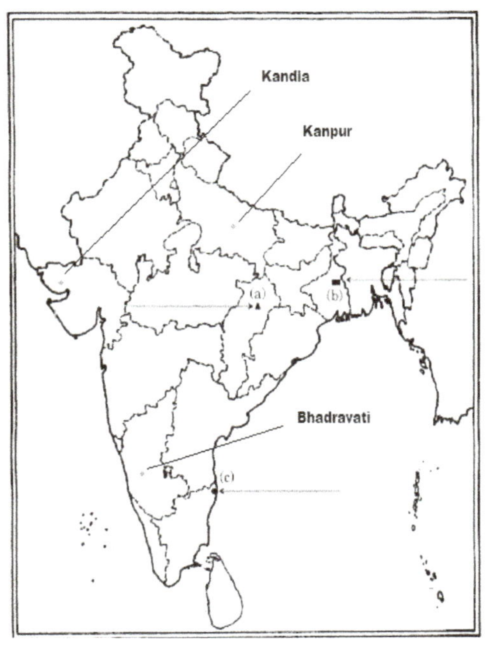

[2]

21.

(*i*) The growing rate of consumption of energy has resulted in the country becoming increasingly dependent on fossils fuels such as coal, oil and gas which are finite. That's why the need for sustainable energy resources like solar, wind and water.   [1]

(*ii*) Renewable energy sources are infinitely cheaper than the conventional ones and are available in the nature in abundance as compared to the non-renewable sources of energy and their ever-rising prices and shortages.   [1]

(*iii*) The uncertainties about the non-renewable sources of energy and their rising prices pose a threat to security of energy supply in future. This in turn leads to uncertainty regarding the future of the national economy and can have serious repercussions.   [1]

(*iv*) There is a phenomenal rise in the prices of oil and gas because of their undisputed demand.   [1]

(*v*) The environment is getting harmed due to increasing use of fossil fuels. It is causing serious environmental problems like pollution and degradation of soil, water and air. On the other hand, renewable energy sources, which are natural sources of energy, are pollution free and eco friendly.   [1]

22. The most abundantly available fossil fuel in India is coal. The different forms of coal are Peat, Lignite, Bituminous and Anthracite. Let's talk about their importance in detail: [1]

(*i*) Peat : Decaying plants in swamps produce peat and it is burnt as fuel or applied to the soil to improve the texture and moisture. [1]

(*ii*) Lignite: It is brown is colour, soft and has high moisture content. Generation of electricity is the main usage of lignite. [1]

(*iii*) Bituminous: It's usually black in colour and has medium heat per kg. It is used for producing coke.   [1]

(*iv*) Anthracite: The carbon content in per kg is more than 90%. It is used in residential and commercial space heating.   [1]

23. Need to conserve mineral resources are:

(*i*) Mineral resources are limited and non-renewable.   [1]

(*ii*) All minerals are not evenly distributed on the earth surface so it will take time to find all the minerals.   [1]

(*iii*) The geological processes of mineral formation are very slow but the rate of consumption is very high.   [1]

Mineral resources can be conserved by following ways:

(i) There should be planned usage of these resources. [0.5]

(ii) Bicycle or walk through can be used as a means of transport to travel short distances. Judious and proper uses of minerals should be promoted by government means like as rebate in personal tax for a person who use sustainable means for his transportation or other work . [0.5]

(iii) Switch off the vehicles engines at railway crossing or at a red traffic light. [0.5]

(iv) The government should implement some strict usage law in order to conserve these resources. [0.5]

MULTIPLE CHOICE QUESTIONS

1. What is a mineral ?
   (a) Naturally formed aggregate of minute particles
   (b) A naturally occurring substance that has a definite chemical composition.
   (c) Heterogeneous naturally occurring substance with a definable internal structure.
   (d) None of these

2. Limestone is an example of......
   (a) Metallic minerals
   (b) Manganese ore
   (c) Non-metallic minerals
   (d) None of these

3. Copper is used in making....
   (a) Utensils
   (b) Buildings
   (c) Cricket equipment
   (d) Both *(b)* and *(c)*

4. What type of energy is obtained from coal, petroleum and natural gas?
   (a) Hydro energy
   (b) Thermal energy
   (c) Renewable energy
   (d) Solar energy

5. Shrubs, farm wastes, animal and human wastes are used to produce.......
   (a) Rocks   *(b)* Minerals
   (c) Biogas   *(d)* Cotton

   1. *(b)*   2. *(c)*   3. *(a)*   4. *(b)*   5. *(c)*

FILL IN THE BLANKS

1. A ____________ studies the formation of minerals, their age and physical and chemical properties.

2. a wide range of colours , hardness, crystal forms, lustre and density is found in minerals due to ______________ and _____________ conditions

3. Odisha was the largest ____________ producing state in India in 2009-10.

4. Iron ore is transported as slurry through ______________

5. ____________ is the oldest oil producing State of India.

Solutions

1. Geologist
2. Physical, chemical
3. Bauxite
4. Pipelines
5. Assam

TRUE OR FALSE

1. Copper is mainly used in electrical cables and electronic industries
2. Nagarcoil and Jaisalmer are well known for effective use of solar energy
3. Minerals occur in beds or layers in sedimentary rocks.
4. Mumbai high is an offshore oil field?
5. Koderma, in Jharkhand is the leading producer of Bauxite

Solutions

1. True
2. False
3. True
4. True
5. False

Manufacturing Industries

Summary

Manufacturing Industries

Introduction

- Production of goods in large quantities after processing from raw materials to more valuable products.
- The economic strength of a country is measured by the development of manufacturing industries.
- Manufacturing industries helps in modernising agriculture.
- It reduces the heavy dependence of people on agriculture income by providing them jobs.
- Helps in bringing down regional disparities.

Location

- The industrial locations are complex in nature.
- It depends on the availability of raw material.
- Cost of production at site.
- Closeness to market.
- Availability of transport.
- Availability of cheap labours.
- Government policies

Classification

On the basis of raw material sources

Agro Based Industries - Cotton textile, jute textile, sugar and vegetable oil

Mineral Based Industries - iron and steel, petrochemical, aluminium and cement industries.

One the basis of their main role

- Basic or key industries-supply their products to manufacture other goods, ex. Iron and steel and copper smelting .
- Consumer industries—produce goods for direct use of consumers. Ex-sugar, toothpaste, paper, soap etc.

On the basis of capital investment

- Small scale industries-owned and run by individuals having small number of labourers .
- Large Scale Industry-Industries having large number of labourers and employs in each unit.
- Investment is more than one crore Rs, Cotton or jute textile industries are large scale industries

On the basis of ownership

- Private Sector Industries-owned by individuals or firms such as Bajaj Auto or TISCO situated at Jamshedpur are called private sector industries.
- Public Sector Industries-owned by the state and its agencies like Bharat Heavy Electricals Ltd., or Bhilai Steel Plant or Durgapur Steel Plant are public sector industries.
- Joint Sector Industries-owned jointly by the private firms and the state or its agencies such as Gujarat Alkalies Ltd., or Oil India Ltd. fall in the group of joint sector industries.
- Co-operative Sector Industries-owned and run co-operatively by a group of people who are generally producers of raw materials of the given industry such as a sugar mill owned and run by farmers are called co-operative sector industries.

Agro based industries

Textile industry

- It contributes 14 percent in industrial production and provides employment to 35 million peoples directly.
- It contributes 4 percent towards GDP.
- It is self reliant industries, which complete in the value chain.

Cotton industries

- There are nearly 1600 cotton and human made fibre textile mills in the country. 80 percent of mills in private sector and rest in public sector.
- It is concentrated in cotton belt of Maharashtra and Gujarat.
- It supports many other industries like chemical and dyes, mill stores, packaging materials and engineering works.
- The handspun khadi provide large scale employment to weavers in their homes.
- India export yarn to Japan.
- It has second largest installed capacity of spindles in the world next to China.
- There is need to upgrade machinery in the weaving and processing sector.

Jute Textiles

- India is the largest producer of raw jute and jute goods and stand at second place after Bangladesh.
- Due to availability of ideal condition most of the jute mills located in the bank of Hugli river of west Bengal.
- There are about 70 jute mills in India, which supports 2.61 lakh workers directly and another 40 lakh small and marginal farmers are engaged in cultivation for raw material i.e Mesta or Jute.
- To increase in productivity,and to improve quality,the national Jute policy was formulated
- The main market of jute textiles are U.S.A, Canada, Russia, U.K and Australia.

Sugar industries

- India is second largest producer of sugar and stand first in Gur and Khandsari production.
- There are 460 sugar mills in India spread in U.P, Bihar, M.P, Punjab and Harayana.
- Recent year the sugar industries shifted in Maharashtra due to idea condition of growing sugarcane.

Minerals based industries

Iron and steel industries

- It is categorized in heavy industry.
- India stands at ninth rank among world in crude steel production with 32.8 ton steel production in a year.
- In spite of large quantity of production per capita consumption of steel is only 32 kg per annum.
- Steel authority of India, market the steel of all public sector, where TISCO market its produce through Tata Steel.
- The presence of iron and steel industries is mainly found in Chotanagpur plateau region.

Aluminium smelting

- Second most metallurgical industries in India .
- To manufacture aircraft, utensils and wires, it is used.
- India have eight smelting plant.
- Bauxite is the raw materials used in the smelters.

Chemical industries

- It contributes 3 percent of the GDP.
- Third largest in Asia and 12th in world in production.
- It includes small and large manufacturing industries.
- It includes petrochemicals which are used for manufacturing of synthetic fibres, synthetic rubbers plastics, dye stuffs etc.

Fertiliser industry

- It includes the production of nitrogenous fertilizer, mainly Urea, DAP and NPK.
- India is the third largest producer of nitrogenous fertilizers.
- There are fifty seven fertilizers units in India and one cooperative is in Hazira located in Gujarat.

Cement industries

- The first cement plant was setup in Chennai in 1904.

- There are 128 large plants and 332 mini plants in the country.

Information technology

- Due to development of IT in Banglore it is known as Electronic capital of India.
- Eighteen software technology parks provide single window service and high data communication facility to software experts.
- Up to 31 march 2015, it employed over one million person.
- BPOs has emerged as the medium of foreign earning .
- The innovation and development in the hardware and software, the IT industries rising continuously.

Industrial Pollution and Environmental Degradation

Industries contributes in the development and growth of the economy but also caused in the unbalance of nature, caused contamination of resources.

Types of Pollution

- Air - caused by undesirable gases such as sulphur dioxide and carbon monoxide, air borne particles such as dust, sprays, mist & smoke.
- Water Pollution - Caused by organic & inorganic industrial wastes such as release of lead, mercury pesticides, fertilizers, synthetic chemical, plastics, rubber, fly ash, phosphogypsum etc.
- Thermal Pollution - Caused by nuclear power plants nuclear & weapon production cause cancers birth defects & miscarriages.
- Noise Pollution - Causes heaving impairment, increased heart rate & blood pressure by making unwanted noise.

Control of Environment Degradation

- Minimising the use of water by reusing recycling.
- Harvesting rainwater to meet water requirement.
- Treatment of hot water and effluents before releasing in ponds & rivers, involves 3 steps.

    1. Primary treatment by mechanical means.

    2. Secondary treatment by biological process.

    3. Tertiary treatment by biological chemical & physical processes.

Points to know

Agglomeration economy

When a number of companies establish their units at one place to avail maxim benefits nearby the population, both industries and people gets opportunity to develop.

GDP

Gross domestic product.

EMS

Environment management system

PREVIOUS YEARS' EXAMINATION QUESTIONS

▶ 1 Mark Questions

1. **Which one of the following has been the major source of foreign exchange for IT industry?**

    (a) BHEL

    (b) SAIL

    (c) BPO

    (d) OIL

    [TERM 2, 2011]

2. **Which one of the following factors plays the most important role in the location of an industry in a particular region?**

    (a) Raw material

    (b) Market

    (c) Least production cost

    (d) Transport

    [TERM 2, 2012]

▶ 3 Mark Questions

3. **Explain any three problems faced by Iron and Steel Industry in India.**

    [TERM 2, 2011]

4. **Describe any three factors that control industrial location.**

    [TERM 2, 2011]

5. **How do industries pollute air? Explain ill effects of pollution.**

    [TERM 2, 2012]

6. Why was cotton textile industry concentrated in the cotton growing belt of Maharashtra and Gujarat in the early years? Explain any three reasons.

[TERM 2, 2012]

7. Locate and label the following items with appropriate symbols and write their correct names on the same map:

(*i*) Durgapur - Iron and Steel Plant

(*ii*) Kaiga - Nuclear Power Plant

(*iii*) Vishakhapatnam - Sea Port

[TERM 2, 2012]

8. Why has the 'Chhota Nagpur Plateau Region' the maximum concentration of iron and steel industries? Analyse the reason.

[TERM 2, 2015]

9. Suggest any three steps to minimize the environmental degradation caused by the industrial development in India.

[TERM 2, 2016]

▷ 5 Mark Questions

10. Explain any five measures to control industrial pollution in India.

[TERM 2, 2013]

11. What is the manufacturing sector? Why is it considered the backbone of development? Interpret the reason.

[TERM 2, 2015]

✎ Solutions

1. (*c*) BPO   [1]

2. (*c*) Least production cost   [1]

3. The Iron and Steel Industry is a basic industry since all the other industries are dependent on it for their machinery.

Problems faced by Iron and Steel Industry in India are:

(*i*) High costs and capital.   [1]

(*ii*) Limited availability of cooking coal and irregular supply of energy.   [1]

(*iii*) Labour productivity is low.   [1]

(*iv*) Poor Infrastructure for setting up industries.

4. The factors that control industrial location are:

(*i*) Availability of raw materials and low capital cost.   [1]

(*ii*) Proximity or closeness to the markets. [1]

(*iii*) Availability of cheap and skilled labour. [1]

(*iv*) Government policies.

5. Industries pollute air by emitting high proportion of undesirable gases like sulphur dioxide and carbon monoxide.

The ill effects of pollution are as follows:

(*i*) It adversely affects human health causing respiratory and water borne diseases.   [1]

(*ii*) It degrades the environment and increases the amount of carbon dioxide causing global warming   [1]

(*iii*) It causes loss of habitat for plants and animals.   [1]

6. Cotton textile industry was concentrated in Maharashtra and Gujarat in the early years due to:

(*i*) The availability of raw cotton.   [1]

(*ii*) The availability of market, labour, transport including accessible port facilities.   [1]

(*iii*) Suitable moist climate for cultivation of cotton.   [1]

7.
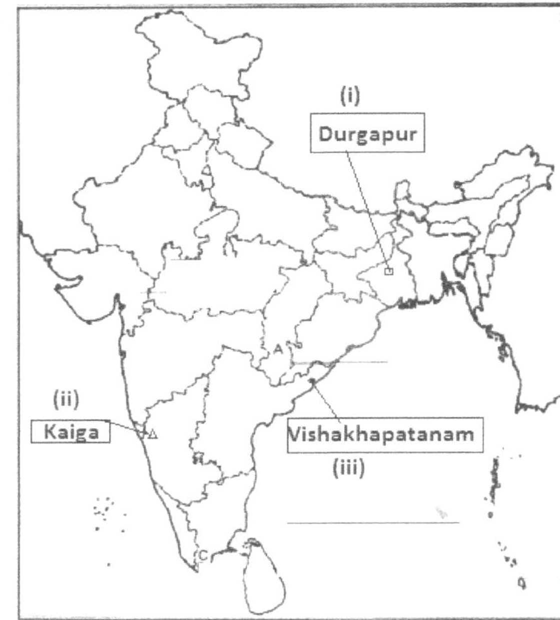

[1 + 1 + 1]

8. Chhotanagpur plateau region has the maximum concentration of iron and steel industries because of the below reasons:

    1. Region is rich in low cost iron ore   [1]
    2. High grade raw material in proximity   [1]
    3. Cheap labour and vast growth potential in the home market.   [1]

9. The industrial development contributes to the economic growth but it also affect the environment. Industries are responsible for degradation in air, water, land etc.

    We can reduce environmental degradation caused by industries by the following ways:-

    (i) Minimizing used water for processing by reusing and recycling it in two or more successive stages.   [1]

    (ii) Water requirement can be met by rain water harvesting   [1]

    (iii) By dumping, sewage and industries wastage in remote areas from urban population.

    [1]

    (iv) Degradration in air can be reduced by using oil or gas instead of coal in factories. Pollution check certificates should be made compulsory for factories to operate and function.

10. Five measures to control industrial pollution in India are as follows:

    (i) Particulate matter in the air can be reduced by fitting smoke stacks to factories with electrostatic precipitators, fabric filters, scrubbers and inertial separators.   [1]

    (ii) Smoke can be reduced by using oil or gas instead of coal in factories. Pollution check certificates should be made compulsory for factories to operate and function.   [1]

    (iii) Machinery and equipments adopting the latest technology can be used and the existing equipments should be upgraded. Generators should be fitted with silencers.

    (iv) Waste generation can be minimized by using ash through ash pond management, ash water recycling system and liquid waste management.   [1]

    (v) Afforestation should be encouraged and green belts should be set up around factories to maintain ecological balance.   [1]

11. In the manufacturing sector, raw products are transferred in to more valuable products, so it is also known as secondary sector. It is considered the backbone of development for the given reasons: [1]

    (i) It provides materials like fertilizers, pesticides to the agricultureal sector.   [1]

    (ii) It creates job opportunities, as a large portion of population is dependent on agriculture which leads to disguised unemployment.   [1]

    (iii) The export of manufactured goods expands trade and thus adds to foreign exchange.   [1]

    (iv) It also minimizes the regional differences, when an industry is being set up in the tribal or remote areas.   [1]

    (v) It plays an major role in eradicating poverty. It also helps in modernizing agriculture, which forms the backbone of our economy.

MULTIPLE CHOICE QUESTIONS

1. What are Public Sector Industries?
    (a) Industries which are owned and operated by private agencies
    (b) Industries which are owned and operated by government agencies
    (c) Industries which are owned and operated by individuals
    (d) Industries which are owned and operated by government and private agencies

2. Where was the first cement plant established in India?
    (a) Kerala
    (b) Assam
    (c) Chennai
    (d) Maharashtra

3. AMUL is an example of…..
    (a) Cooperative Sector Industry
    (b) Agro-based industry
    (c) Mining industry
    (d) Heavy industry

4. To which one of the following countries does India export jute goods?
    (a) Japan   (b) China
    (c) USA   (d) France

5. The pollution caused by the discharge of hot water from factories and thermal plants into rivers and ponds before cooling is called as......

   (*a*) Air pollution

   (*b*) Thermal pollution

   (*c*) Water pollution

   (*d*) Soil pollution

Answer Keys

1. (*b*)   2. (*c*)   3. (*a*)   4. (*c*)   5. (*b*)

FILL IN THE BLANKS

1. _______________ is the backbone of any country's economy

2. NMCC stands for _____________________.

3. Sugar is an example of ___________ industry

4. Sulphuric acid, nitric acid, alkalis, soda ash and caustic soda are ___________ types of chemicals.

5. The major drawback of cotton industry is ___________________ .

Solutions

1. Steel production

2. National Manufacturing Competitiveness Council

3. Agro-based

4. Inorganic

5. Fragmented nature of cotton processing

TRUE OR FALSE

1. Chhota Nagpur region maximum concentration of iron and steel industries

2. Industries do not cause environmental degradation

3. NTPC markets steel for the public sector plants.

4. Agriculture and industry are complementary to each other.

5. Banglore has emerged as the electronic capital of India..

Solutions

1. True

2. False

3. False

4. True

5. True

Life Lines of National Economy

Summary

Means of Transport

Roadways

- Road networks of India is largely developed in the world.
- The cost of construction of roads is lower.
- Roads can cross relatively more dismembered and undulating geology.
- Roads can arrange higher inclinations of slant and in that capacity can navigate mountains.
- Door to door services can provide easily with the help of roads.
- In state PWD, in districts zila parisad, in rural area maintains the roads.

Golden Quadrilateral Super Highways

- a major road development project launched to connect Delhi, Kolkata-Chennai- Mumbai and Delhi by six-lane super highways by Indian government.
- Srinagar of Jammu & Kashmir and Kanyakumari of Tamilnadu connects with North-South corridors.
- The Silcher of Assam and Porbander of Gujarat connecting by the East-West Corridor .
- To minimize the distance and travelling time is the main goal to link.

Railways

- Railway is the largest public sector undertaking in the country.
- The distribution pattern of the railway network in the country has been largely influence by physiographic, economic and administrative factors.

- The Himalyan mountains regions are unfavourable for the construction of railway lines due to high relief sparse population & each of economic opportunities.
- The northern plains provide most favourable condition having high population density.
- Rivers also create problem for lay down of railway tracts.

Water ways

- Waterways are the cheapest way of transport.
- The Ganga river between Allahabad and Haldia, which cover 1620 km is national waterways.
- The brahmputra river between Sadiya and Dhubri covering 891 km distance is national waterways.
- 95 percent of the country trade is done by sea.

Means of communication

- The personal communication and mass communication including television, radio, press, etc. are the major means of communication.
- India postal network is the largest means of the communication in the world.
- India have one of the largest telecom network in the Asia.
- Doordarshan is the national television of India.
- In India about 100 language newspaper is published.
- India is the largest producer of feature films in the world.

International Trade and Tourism

- The exchange of goods among people; states & countries is referred to as trade.
- Export or import of goods and services between two and more than two countries termed as International Trade.

- Exports and imports are the components of trade. The balance of a trade of a country is the difference between its export and import.
- When the value of exports exceeds the value of imports, it is called favourable balance of trades.

Tourism as a Trade

- Tourism has proved itself as one of the most important aspect of trade.
- Tourism in India has grown substantially. National integration has encouraged it.
- Provide support to local handicrafts.
- Provides support to cultural pursuits.
- Develops of international understanding about our culture and heritage.

Points to know

Pradhan Mantri Gramin Sadak Yojna

The Pradhan Mantri Gram Sadak Yojana is a nationwide plan in India to provide good all-weather road connectivity to unconnected villages.

STD

Subscriber Trunk Dialing

PREVIOUS YEARS' EXAMINATION QUESTIONS

▷ 1 Mark Questions

1. Which one of the following major ports has been developed to decongest Kolkata port?

    (a) Kandla   (b) Haldia

    (c) Paradip   (d) Marmagao

    [TERM 2, 2011]

2. Which one of the following is an inland riverine port?

    (a) Kandla A   (b) Kolkata

    (c) Mumbai   (d) Tuticorin

    [TERM 2, 2012]

3. Which one of the following ports is the biggest with a spacious, natural and well sheltered harbor?

    (a) Kolkata   (b) Chennai

    (c) Mumbai   (d) Vishakhapatnam

    [TERM 2, 2013]

4. Name the river related to National Waterways No. 2.

    [TERM 2, 2017]

▷ 3 Mark Questions

5. Explain the importance of railways as the principal mode of transportation for freight and passengers in India. [TERM 2, 2015]

6. Examine with example the role of means of transport and communication in making our life prosperous and comfortable.

    [TERM 2, 2017]

▷ 4 Mark Questions

7. Mention any two inland waterways of India. Write three characteristics of each.

    [TERM 2, 2011]

8. "Dense and efficient network of transport and communication is a pre- requisite for national and international trade." Support the statement with four arguments.

    [TERM 2, 2012, DELHI 2018]

▷ 5 Mark Questions

9. Describe any five major problems faced by road transport in India. [TERM 2, 2013]

10. "Advancements of international trade of a country is an index to its prosperity." Support the statement with suitable examples.

    [TERM 2, 2014]

11. Classify communication services into two categories? Explain main features of each.

    [TERM 2, 2016]

12. "Roadways still have an edge over railways in India." Support the statement with arguments.

    [TERM 2, 2016]

⚿ Solutions

1. (b) Haldia [1]
2. (b) Kolkata [1]
3. (c) Mumbai [1]
4. Brahmaputra is related to National Waterways No. 2. [1]
5. For transportation of freight and passengers in India, Indian Railways is the principle mode. People can conduct various activities like sightseeing, business and pilgrimage with the transportation of goods over long distances. [1]

    It is helping the country to accelerate the development as well as bind the economic life of the industry and agriculture for the country.

    For the current scenario, Railways is the largest public sector undertaking in the country. [1]

6. Means of transport and communication plays an important role in making our life prosperous and comfortable in following ways:

   (*i*) Now it is easy to export and import good because of means of transport and it helps in the economic development of the country, which helps in raising living standard of peoples [1]

   (*ii*) People of different regions and different cultures are connected to each other via the internet and mobile phones. People are aware of what is happening in the world. [1]

   (*iii*) It helps in the fast development of the country which requires advance means of communication and transport. It is easier to travel long distances in very short time, which paced the globalization. For example, in case of a storm, the governments can inform people so that they can ensure their safety. [1]

7. Two inland waterways of India are:

   (*i*) The Brahmaputra River between Sadiya and Dhubri. [1]

   (*ii*) The Ganga River between Allahabad and Haldia. [1]

   Three characteristics of The Brahmaputra River between Sadiya and Dhubri are: [1]

   (*i*) It is also known as National Waterway 2.

   (*ii*) Its length is 891km.

   (*iii*) It facilitates national security and is used as transportation link between states.

   Three characteristics of The Ganga River between Allahabad and Haldia: [1]

   (*i*) It is known as National Waterway 1.

   (*ii*) It is 1,620km long.

   (*iii*) It provides pilgrimage opportunities.

8. Dense and efficient network of transport and communication is a pre-requisite for national and international trade because:

   (*i*) Raw materials can easily reach their respective centres of production by means of good transportation. [1]

   (*ii*) Good transport infrastructure is very important to enable finished products to reach their respective markets. [1]

   (*iii*) Communication eases the integration of markets and investments. [1]

   (*iv*) Communication facilities are of utmost importance in tertiary activities like providing knowledge about events happening in distant places. [1]

9. Five major problems faced by road transport in India are:

   (*i*) India is a densely populated country and the road network is inadequate and incapable in catering to the needs of such a large population. [1]

   (*ii*) Volume of traffic is the biggest problem as the number of vehicles is too much in India and it often leads to traffic jams. [1]

   (*iii*) More than half of the roads in India are unmetalled and this reduces its usage during the rainy season. The roads become slippery and very difficult to drive on. [1]

   (*iv*) National highways are made for travelling on long routes but they are less than the situation demands. Also, many highways need upgrading as they are too old and not safe for driving. [1]

   (*v*) Casual attitude of the citizens towards the traffic rules is also a major cause of traffic jams and accidents. [1]

10. "Advancements of international trade of a country is an index to its prosperity."

    (*i*) India has been earning large foreign exchange through the export of information technology in the recent years and it has thus appeared to become a software giant at the international level. [1]

    (*ii*) International trade contributes to India's economic growth, raising income level of people and has helped India to improve its productivity of manufactured goods. [1]

    (*iii*) There are many goods or resources possessed by one country and are required by other and vice-versa. These differences create conditions for international trade as the resources are limited and no country can survive without International trade. [1]

    (*iv*) Apart from goods and services, in the recent years, exchange of commodities and goods have also been superseded by the exchange of information and knowledge. [1]

    Thus, it can be concluded that advancement of international trade of a country is an index of its economic prosperity.

11. The two main categories in which communication can be divided into are Personal communication and mass communication. [1]

    Personal communication can be understood as exchange of communication in between two people. [1]

The Indian postal network is the largest in the world. It handles written communication as well as parcels. [1]

Mass communication creates awareness and provides entertainment among people about various national programmes and policies. It includes radio, television and newspaper, magazines, books and films. [1 + 1]

12. **India has a road network of about 2.3 million km which is one of the largest road networks in the world.**

"Roadways still have an edge over railways in India." can be supported by the following reasons:

(*i*) **Money spent on road construction is much lower in comparison to railway lines.** [1]

(*ii*) **Roads can be covered and can be comparatively more anatomized.** [1]

(*iii*) **It can cover traverse mountains and higher gradients of slopes such as the Himalayas.** [1]

(*iv*) **It is an economical mode of transportation for small amount of goods and for a few people over shorter distances.** [1]

(*v*) **It can also lower the cost of loading and unloading as it provides door-to-door service.** [1]

(*vi*) **It is also used as a linkage between railway stations, sea ports and air ports so it acts as a feeder to other modes of transport.**

MULTIPLE CHOICE QUESTIONS

1. Which one of the following is the most important modes of transportation in India ?
   - (*a*) Pipeline
   - (*b*) Railways
   - (*c*) Roadways
   - (*d*) Airways

2. In which language is the maximum number of newspapers published in India
   - (*a*) Hindi
   - (*b*) English
   - (*c*) Telugu
   - (*d*) Punjabi

3. Which of these was the first port developed soon after Independence?
   - (*a*) Surat
   - (*b*) Goa
   - (*c*) Kamarajar Port
   - (*d*) Kandla

4. Which of these is a super highway?
   - (*a*) Sher Shah Suri Marg
   - (*b*) Golden Quadrilateral
   - (*c*) Jawaharlal Nehru port
   - (*d*) National Highway-12

5. Which communication service in India is the largest in the world?
   - (*a*) Railways
   - (*b*) Airways
   - (*c*) Postal
   - (*d*) Waterways

Answer Keys

1. (*b*)   2. (*a*)   3. (*d*)   4. (*b*)   5. (*c*)

FILL IN THE BLANKS

1. Jawaharlal Nehru port developed to _____________.

2. The air transport was nationalised in_____

3. __________________ airport is situated in Mumbai.

4. __________________ have a length of 14,500 km

5. Indian railways lack ____________________.

Solutions

1. Decongest the Mumbai port and serve as a hub port for the region
2. 1953
3. Chhatrapati Shivaji
4. Inland Waterways
5. Repair and maintenance of tracks and bridges

TRUE OR FALSE

1. Border Roads Organisation was established in 1960.
2. National highways are laid and maintained by the CPWD.
3. HVJ pipeline is 1700 Km long
4. Difference between the total value of exports and imports is called balance of payment.
5. Tourism trade brings in much needed foreign exchange.

Solutions

1. True
2. Trie
3. False
4. False
5. True

Unit III : Political Science

Political Parties

Summary

Political parties-An introduction and role

- A group of people who agree with some dogma or tenets and contest elections with the goal of formation of government.

- Their dogma and tenets for the development and welfare of society .

- All parties try to impress people for their support by comparing their policies from with other political parties

- They seek to implement these policies by wining popular support through elections.

- A basic political division of a society is reflected by the parties. Being a part of a society ,parties involves in Partisanship.

- Party is known by his dogma, policies which they support and by whom they associated.

- A political party has three components (*i*) the leaders (*ii*) the active members, and (*iii*) the followers.

- Parties contest elections.

- The candidates for contesting in elections are opted by the top most leaders of parties .

- A party reduces a vast multitude of opinions into a few basic positions which it supports.

- The major decisions are taken by political executive that formed by political parties after winning election and forming government .

- Parties recruit leaders train them and then make them ministers to run the government in the

- Those parties that lose in the elections play the role of opposition to the parties in power, by voicing different views and criticizing government for its failures or wrong policies.

- public opinion is shaped by parties. Issue is raised and highlighted by parties .

- Many of the pressure groups are the augmentation of political gatherings among various areas of society.

- Parties here and there likewise dispatch developments for the determination of issues looked by individuals.

Types of Party System.

One-Party System

- In some countries only one party is allowed to control and run government. These are called one-party system.

- In China only the Communist party is allowed to rule. Although, legally speaking, people are free to form political parties.

- We cannot consider one party system as a good option.

- Any democratic system must allow at least two parties to compete in elections and provide a fair change for the competing parties to come to power.

Two-Party System

- In some countries power usually changes between two main parties. Several other parties may exist, contest elections and win a few seats in the national legislatures.

- If only the two main parties have a serious chance of winning majority of seats to form government, such a party system is called two-party system.

- In United Kingdom and USA the two-party system.

Multi-Party system

- When the two parties have a reasonable chance of coming to power either on their own strength or in alliance with others, is termed as a multiparty system.

- In India, we have multi-party system, the governments is formed by various parties coming together in a coalition.

- When several parties in a multiparty system join hands the purpose of contesting elections and winning power it is termed as alliance or a front

- The multi-party system often appears very messy and leads to political instability.

- At the same time, this system allows a variety of interests and opinions to enjoy political representation.

National and regional parties.

National Political Parties

- The national political parties have their units in various states. But by and large all these units follows the same policies, programmes and strategy that is decided at the national level.

- Election Commission provide recognition to every political parties by registering them. The Commission treats all parties equally, some special facilities is provided to large and established parties.

- The criteria to be registered National Party is to get at least 6 percent total votes in Lok Sabha elections or Assembly elections in four states and wins at least four seats in the Lok Sabha.

- six national recognised parties in the country in 2006.

- Indian national congress founded in 1885,build moder secular democratic republic under the leadership of Jawahar Lal Nehru.

- it emerged as the largest party with 145 member in Loksabha election held in 2004.

- BJP founded in 1980 want to bulid a strong and modern India by following ancient culture and value. Hindutatva is an important element in its conception.

- It came in power in 1998 as NDA but lost in 2004. currently it is in power.

- BSP Kanshi Ram founded in 1984,it upholds the dalits, adivasis, OBC's and religious minorities.

- It believes in the ideas of Oyotiba Phule and Naiker and follows their tenets.

- It has its main base in U.P and substantial presence in Delhi, Punjab.

- Communist Party of India (Marxist), is founded in 1964.

- It based on Marxism-Leninism,enjoy,it is in strong majority in West Bengal, Kerala and Tripura have impact among the factories worker,farmers, and labourers.

- In Bengal, it is in power more than 30 years without break.

- Communist Party of India (CPI) formed in 1925 based on the ideology of Marxism–Leninism.

- It accepts democracy as the means of the promoting the interest of working class.it is split in 1964.

- National congress party due to split in congress party in 1999 NCP is formed.Peoples Maharashtra ,Meghalaya and Assam have strong feeling with it.

Regional parties

- The Election commission registered a party as a National party which gets at least 6 per cent of the total votes in an election of the State and wins at least two seats.. Eg Samajwadi party,Janta dal, Samta Dal

- State parties generally reffered as Regional Political Party. It exists, operates and functions at the regional level.

- It gives importance to state related issues, specific problems of the region and it has great influence only on the people of that region.

Challenges faced by Political parties and reforms.

Challenges faced by Political parties

Lack of internal democracy within parties. It is found in parties of all over the world.

- The concentration of power in one or few leaders at the top Parties do not have open list of its members.

- Parties do not hold its routine organisational meetings, fail to conduct its internal elections regularly and refuse to share information.

- Ordinary members of the party do not get sufficient information on what happens inside the party.

- Since one a few leaders exercise paramount power in the party, those who disagree with leadership find it difficult to continue in the party.

- More than loyalty to party principles and policies, personal loyalty to the leader becomes more important.

  Challenge of Dynastic succession relates to the first one. Since most political parties do not practice open and transparent procedures for their functioning.

- There are very few ways for an ordinary worker to rise to the top in a party. Those who happen to be the leaders are in a position of unfair advantage to favour people close to them or even their family members.

- In many parties, the top positions are always controlled by members of the one family.

- They do not have adequate experience or popular support come to occupy positions of power. It is oftenly seen in India.

- The growing role of money and muscle power in parties especially during elections. Since parties are focussed only on winning elections, they tend to use short-cuts to win elections.

- They tend to nominate those candidates who have or can raise lots of money. Rich people and companies who given funds to the parties tend to have influence on the policies and decisions of the party

- In some cases parties support criminals who can win elections.

- voters are not provided a meaningful choice by parties.

Reforms

The constitution was amended to prevent elected MLAs and MPs from changing parties.

- This was done to stop indulging in defection.

- This new law has helped bring defection down. At the same time this has made any dissent even more difficult.

The Supreme Court passed an order to reduce the influence of money and criminals.

- Now it is mandatory for every candidate who contests elections to fill an affidavit giving details of his property and criminal cases pending against him.

- The new system has made a lot of information available to the public. But there is no system of check if the information given by the candidates is true.

  Hold organisational election and file their income tax return.

- The election commission passed an order making it necessary for political parties to hold their organisation elections and file their income tax returns.

- The parties have started doing so, sometimes only in formality. It is not clear if this step has led to greater internal democracy in political parties.

- Beside these many suggestions are often made to reform political parties especially reservation of women in parties.

- Strong law should be to regulate internal affairs of party.

Points to know

PARTISAN

A person strongly committed to a party group or faction .

LEFTIST PARTIES

Having radical, ideological conservative nature

OPPOSITION

The political party or group of parties who failed to make their own government and working as a criticiser of a government.

DEFECTION

Changing party allegiance from the party on which a person get elected to a different party

PREVIOUS YEARS'
EXAMINATION QUESTIONS

▶ 1 Mark Questions

1. The political party which believes in Marxism-Leninism is
   (a) Nationalist Congress Party
   (b) Communist Party of India
   (c) Dravida Munnetra Kazhagam(DMK)
   (d) Bahujan Samaj Party
   [TERM 2, 2011]

2. Which one of the following countries has one party system?
   (a) China   (b) Indo-China
   (c) Japan   (d) Germany
   [TERM 2, 2013]

3. Why do political parties involve partisanship?
   [TERM 2, 2015]

4. Distinguish between pressure groups and political parties by stating any one point of distinction.
   [TERM 2, 2016]

5. Why did India adopt multi-party system?
   [TERM 2, 2016]

▶ 3 Mark Questions

6. Explain how the relationship between political parties and pressure groups can take different forms.
   [TERM 2, 2011]

7. Why can't modern democracies exist without political parties? Explain any three reasons.
   [TERM 2, 2012]

8. Explain the three steps taken by the different authorities to reform political parties and their leaders in India.
   [TERM 2, 2012]

9. Name the national political party which gets inspiration from India's ancient culture and values. Mention four features of that party.
   [TERM 2, 2013]

10. What is meant by regional political party? State the condition required to be recognized as a 'regional political party'.
    [TERM 2, 2016]

▶ 4 Mark Questions

11. Explain how dynastic succession is a major challenge for political parties in India.
    [TERM 2, 2011, 2015]

▶ 5 Mark Questions

12. "About hundred years ago there were few countries that had hardly any political party. Now there are few countries that do not have political parties." Examine this statement.
    [TERM 2, 2014]

13. What is meant by a political party? Describe the three components of a political party.
    [TERM 2, 2015, 2016]

14. Suggest any five effective measures to reform political parties.
    [TERM 2, 2015]

15. "Political parties are a necessary condition for a democracy". Analyze the statement with examples.
    [TERM 2, 2016]

🔑 Solutions

1. (b) Communist Party Of India   [1]

2. (a) China   [1]

3. Political parties represent basic political divisions in a society. A party is known by which part it stands for, which policies it supports and whose interest it upholds by which they try to convince people for their supports. This reflects fundamental political divisions.   [1]

4. Political party.
   A Political party is a group of people who come together to contest elections and hold power in government.
   Pressure group.
   A pressure group is a group of people, working together to change the policy or to influence the decision of the government by democractic means. Sometimes it is extention of a political party among different sections of society.
   Political party sometimes launches movements for the revolution of problems faced by people. These groups actively participate to create pressure.   [1]

5. India adopted multi-party system because India is a democratic country where all individual are free to make their own party. Any democratic system must allow at least two parties to compete in election and provide a fair chance for the competing parties to come to power. To

ensure the sharing of the power among different section of society based on ideology, tenets, religions etc india adopted the multi party system. [1]

6. The relationship between political parties and pressure groups can take different forms in the following ways. [1]

   Pressure groups are often formed by the politicians and political parties. Most of the Employee trade unions and students organizations in our country are either established by or affiliated to one or the other major political party of the country. Most of the leaders of the pressure groups are also the leaders or activist of any political party. [1]

   Sometimes, political parties grow out of such movements. Due to reform movements of 1930s and 1940s parties like DMK and AIADMK were formed.

   Political parties take up the issues raised by pressure groups, resulting in a change in the policies of the political parties at times. [1]

7. Modern democracies cannot exist without political parties because of the following reasons:

   (i) The political parties provide a platform and representation to various sections of the society. [1]

   (ii) These parties provide a forum for public debates and articulation of different opinions. [1]

   (iii) They also give shape to policies and legislations on the basis of their election manifestos that direct the developmental path of a country. [1]

8. Some steps taken by the different authorities to reform political parties are as follows:

   (i) The Constitution was amended to prevent elected MLAs and MPs from changing their parties. If an MLA or an MP changes parties, he or she will lose the seat in the legislature. [1]

   (ii) The Supreme Court made it important for every candidate who contests elections to file an affidavit by providing details of his/her property and criminal cases pending against him/her. [1]

   (iii) Election Commission has made it necessary for political parties to hold organizational elections to maintain inner party democracy and file their income tax returns. [1]

9. The national political party which gets inspiration from India's ancient culture and values is Bharatiya Janata Party. Four features of BJP are as follows:

   (i) A uniform civil code was promoted for people living in the country, irrespective of different castes and religion and have put ban on religious conversions. [1]

   (ii) The party wants the complete state of Jammu and Kashmir to be integrated with India (both politically and territorially). [1]

   (iii) Cultural nationalism is an important element of its conception of Indian nationhood and politics, BJP wants to build a modern and strong India. [1]

   (iv) The party was founded in 1980 by reviving the previous Bharatiya Jana Sangh.

10. A regional political party is a political party that is recognized and has its influence in a particular state of the nation. [1]

    The condition required to be recognized as a 'regional political party' are:

    (i) The party must have secured at least 6 percent of the total votes polled in all the constituencies of the parliament. [1]

    (ii) The party must win at least one seat from the state in Lok Sabha general elections. [1]

11. Dynastic succession is a major challenge for political parties in India:

    Most political parties do not practice open and transparent functioning procedures. [1]

    In a party, an ordinary worker mostly cannot rise to the top. It has confined the spirit of political parties. Leaders favour the people close to them or their family members and chase the unfair advantage of being in position, which leads the favourism and flatterism in the party. [1 + 1]

    In Dynastic Succession the top most position is always occupied by the members of a family, which is unfair to the other party members. it leds the unexperience leading which always diverts the principles of party . [1]

12. There was a shift from anarchy or imperialism to people's government or democracy about a hundred years ago in various counties. after the French revolution and American independence, colonial countries paced their freedom struggles and formed their own demcractic government, rooting out the imperialism. The starting age of democracy was deepened with improvements especially in sharing of powers in different sections of society, giving rights to express their views. The freedom rights leds the

creation of different section of ideology, in society. People with different ideologies organized themselves for their interest with a firm doctrine to come in power,accepted as party in a country. The deepening of democracy led to the formation of different political parties. [1 + 1 + 1]

The change in the map of world democracy led the formation of political parties based on their views. Today we have few country without democracy. [1 + 1]

13. A group of people who come together to contest elections and hold position in the government is called a political party. [1]

They agree on the same policies, beliefs and programs for the society with a view to promote the collective good. [1]

The three components of a political party are as follows:

(*i*) Leader is the person who has been chosen by all the party members and will have all the responsibility to take decision. [1]

(*ii*) Active members. are the members of the party, who actively participate in all type of activities i.e. meeting, rally, organizing, promotions etc. [1]

(*iii*) Followers. are the people who believe in the particular political party and try to make others believe in their agendas and favorable work for the country. Actually the number of followers of any party gives a clear picture of the future of the party. [1]

14. **Five effective measures to reform political parties are as follows:**

(*i*) Any candidate that has any pending conviction should be barred from contesting election. [1]

(*ii*) All political parties should file income tax and the financial accounts must be audited, with that their accounts must be made public. [1]

(*iii*)Introduction of party hopping law preventing an individual from defecting to another party without seeking fresh mandate from the electorates. [1]

(*iv*) All parties must create positions for women and people with disabilities. there should be a transparent and democratic selection of successors of leaders . [1]

(*v*) Parties must encourage inner party democracy, and thus should have regular elections. [1]

15. **"Political parties are a necessary condition for a democracy".**

The importance of political party is directly linked to the emergence of representative democracies. [0.5]

As societies became large and complex, they also needed some agency to gather different views on various issues and to present these to the government. [0.5]

They needed some ways, to bring various representatives together so that a responsible government could be formed. [0.5]

They needed a mechanism to support or restrain the government, make policies, justify or oppose them. [0.5]

Political parties fulfill these needs that every representative government has.

(*i*) The existence of political parties in a representative democracy allows the democratic machinery to function smoothly and ensures that the country runs as per its policies and ideologies and has a responsive and accountable government. They serve as both policy makers and opposition. [0.5]

(*ii*) Without political parties there would be chaos and turmoil in the society. As societies are becoming larger and more complex, there is a general will for dialogue that has to be facilitated by bringing together of representatives from different parts of a country. Only then can there be a responsible government. [0.5]

(*iii*) If there no political parties, every candidate is going to be an independent candidate and will be accountable to their constituency for what they do in the locality, but no one can then be held accountable for larger issues. [0.5]

(*iv*) Modern form of democracies also need representatives from various political parties to form the government and to keep a check on the ruling party by being in the opposition. [0.5]

(*v*) Political parties are required so that a country is governed as per set ideologies and will be responsible for how the country will be run. They put forward various policies and programmes for the electorate's consideration, they participate in parliamentary legislation process, they form and run governments, they provide people access to government machinery and welfare schemes and shape and articulate public opinion. [1]

MULTIPLE CHOICE QUESTIONS

1. What are the three components of a political party?

   (*a*) The leaders, the passive members and general public

   (*b*) The leaders, the active members, and the followers

   (*c*) Party symbol, Party manifesto, and the followers

   (*d*) None of these

2. Which of these is the most common party system?

   (*a*) One-Party   (*b*) Monarchy

   (*c*) Two-Party   (*d*) Multi-Party

3. Which of these is a major political party in India?

   (*a*) Bahujan Samaj Party

   (*b*) Akhil Bharatiya Ashok Sena

   (*c*) Akhil Bharatiya Dal

   (*d*) Akhil Bharatiya Desh Bhakt Morcha

4. Which autonomous constitutional authority responsible for administering election processes in a country?

   (*a*) Municipal Corporation

   (*b*) UPSC

   (*c*) Election Commission

   (*d*) CAG

5. When was the Communist party of India – Marxist (CPI-M) formed?

   (*a*) 2005   (*b*) 1964

   (*c*) 1857   (*d*) 2000

Answer Keys

   1. (*b*)   2. (*d*)   3. (*a*)   4. (*c*)   5. (*b*)

FILL IN THE BLANKS

1. ___________________is not recognised as a national political party.

2. One party political system not considered a good democratic system because___________________.

3. The guiding philosophy of Bharatiya Janata Party is___________________

4. Nationalist Congress party was formed in ___________________

5. Concentration of power in one or few leaders leads to lack of .... within political party.

Solutions

1. Samajwadi Party

2. It does not support the idea of democracy

3. Cultural nationalism

4. 1999

5. Internal democracy

TRUE OR FALSE

1. Telugu Desam Party is a state party.

2. Political parties do not face the challenge of dynastic succession

3. An important function of political party in India is to contest elections.

4. Political parties play the role of both party in power as well as opposition.

5. Political defection is not a very serious problem faced by political parties in India.

Solutions

1. True

2. False

3. True

4. True

5. False

Outcomes of Democracy

Summary

How do we Assess Democracy's Outcomes.

Points to know

Topic -1. How do we assess democracy's outcomes.

- Democracy is a better form of government.
- Democracy was better it Promotes equality among citizens
- It Enhances the dignity of the individual.
- It Improves the quality of decision-making, and Provides a method to resolve conflicts
- It Allows a room to correct mistakes.
- Democracy is the form of the government it can create conditions for achieving something, the citizens have to take advantage with condition and achieve goals.

Political outcomes.

- In a democracy, we are most concerned with ensuring that people will have the right to choose their rules and people will have control over the rulers.
- Whenever possible and necessary, citizens should be able to participate in decision making that affects them all.
- Democracy should be accountable to the citizen, and responsive to the needs and expectations of the citizens.

- The idea of deliberation and negotiation is a important base of democracy.
- The democratic government will take more time to follow procedures before arriving at a decision
- But because it has followed procedures, its decisions may be both more acceptable to the people and more effective.
- Democracy ensures that decision making will be based on norms and procedures. So a citizen, who wants to know if a decision was taken through the correct procedures, can find this out.
- Anyone has the right and the means to examine the process of decision making. This is known as transparency. Transparency is a best outcome of democracy
- Regular free and fair election; open public debate on major policies and legislations and citizens' right to information about the government and its functioning is the actual performance of democracies.
- Democratic government is people owns government ,it may be slow not always very responsive but it is legitimate government overwhelmed by all over the world.

Economic outcome and Reduction of in equality and poverty

- For the fifty years between 1950 and 2000, dictatorship have slightly higher rate of economic growth.
- Evidence shows that in practice many democracies did not fulfil this expectation.

- The difference between less developed countries with dictatorships and democracies is negligible.
- We can expect democracy not to lag behind dictatorship in the respect of economic development.
- Within democracies there can be very high degrees of inequalities.
- In democratic countries like South Africa and Brazil the top 20 per cent people corned more than 60 per cent of the national income, leaving less than 3 per cent for the bottom 20 per cent population
- Countries like Denmark and Hungary are much better in this respect.

Reduction of in equality and poverty

- democracies are based on political equality ,but due to economic inequality it seems difficult .
- A small number of ultra rich enjoy a highly disproportionate share of wealth and incomes .
- The peoples who are at the bottom of the society loosing their income level and compel to sustain low standard of life.
- Democratic countries do not appear to be successful to reduce poverty but their efforts to reduce inequality can't criticise as the economic disparities depends on many things.

Accomodation of social diversity

- Democracies usually develop a procedure to conduct their competition. This reduces the possibility of these tensions becoming explosive or violent.
- The conflicts among different groups can't be fully solved by any society .
- democracy can successfully handle the social difference, divisions and conflicts.

Majority rule government must satisfy two conditions to accomplish this result

(*i*) It is important to comprehend that vote based system isn't just run by dominant part supposition.

- The greater part in every case needs to work with the minority.
- With the goal that administration capacity to speak to the general view.

(*ii*) It is likewise important that govern by major part does not progress toward becoming guideline by greater part network as far as religion or race or phonetic gathering, and so forth.

- If someone is barred from being in majority on the basis of birth, then the democratic rule ceases to be accommodative for that person or group.

Points to know

MONARCHY

The governing of country is in the hand of the of king, who avails despotic power.

DIGNITY

The word denotes privileged position, honourable rank or importance given to any particular post or personating.

TRANSPARENCY

Right or means to examine the process of decision making.

Points to know

JURISDICTION

The area it may be the geographical boundaries or certain kinds of subject over which someone has legal authority.

COALITION GOVERNMENT

A government in which many or multiple political parties cooperate, reducing the dominance of any one party within that "coalition". The usual reason for this arrangement is that no party on its own can achieve a majority in the legislative body.

PANCHAYAT SAMITI

Mandals, taluka panchayats, block panchayats, or panchayat samiti are rural local governments at the intermediate level in panchayat raj institutions (PRI).

PREVIOUS YEARS'
EXAMINATION QUESTIONS

▷ 1 Mark Questions

1. Which one of the following is not the quality of democracy?

   [TERM 2, 2012]

   (*a*) It promotes equality among citizens

   (*b*) It takes quick decisions

   (*c*) It improves the quality of decision making

   (*d*) It enhances the dignity of the individual

2. Which one of the following features is common to most of the democracies?

   (*a*) They have formal constitution

   (*b*) They hold regular elections

   (*c*) They have political parties

   (*d*) All the above

   [TERM 2, 2013]

▷ 3 Mark Questions

3. Explain the role of democratic governments in reducing economic disparities.

   [TERM 2, 2011]

4. How do democracies accommodate social diversity? Explain.

   [TERM 2, 2011]

5. "An ideal government would not only keep itself away from corruption but also make fighting corruption and black money a top priority". Justify the statement by highlighting the values attached to it.

   [TERM 2, 2014]

6. How is democracy accountable and responsive to the needs and expectations of the citizens? Analyse.

   [TERM 2, 2015]

7. On the basis of which values will it be a fair expectation that democracy should produce a harmonious social life? Explain.

   [TERM 2, 2017]

▷ 5 Mark Questions

8. "Democracy is seen to be good in principle but felt to be not so good in practice". Justify the statement.

   [TERM 2, 2013]

9. "Democracy stands much superior in promoting dignity and freedom of the citizen". Justify the statement.

   [TERM 2, 2016]

10. "Democracies lead to peaceful and harmonious life among citizens." Justify this statement.

    [DELHI 2018]

🔑 Solutions

1. It takes quick decisions [1]

2. (*d*) All the above [1]

3. The government plays an important role in reducing economic disparities by adopting the following measures:

   (*i*) Government provides public facilities to uplift the economically weak class therefore economic gulf between poor and reach can be breached. [1]

   (*ii*) Government undertakes extensive social welfare schemes and strives to achieve universal literacy rate. [1]

   (*iii*) Government takes care to provide equal opportunities to all and answer that the income is eventually distributed among the people [1]

4. **Democracy accommodates social diversity in following ways:**

   (*i*) It allows methods to resolve conflicts. It takes into account views from both Majority and Minority, so as to provide a general view of the situation. [1]

   (*ii*) It allows equality, fair representation to all irrespective of caste, creed, colour, region, religion or language. [1]

   (*iii*) The weaker sections of the society are given the economic benefits to help them improve their living standards and live a dignified life. [1]

5. **"An ideal government would not only keep itself away from corruption but also make fighting corruption and black money a top priority". This can be justified by highlighting values such as legitimacy, responsiveness and accountability:**

   (*i*) Legitimacy – Social evils like Inflation, Poverty and poor political ethics arise from big sources of corruption and black money. A government elected by people is expected to work for their well being and prosperity, and when a government fails to control corruption it loses all its legitimacy to rule. [1]

(ii) Accountability – A government is responsible for management of polity and its resources, whereas corruption and black money always impede the prime allocation of resources. [1]

(iii) Responsiveness – People's representatives who have the mandates of people of their constituencies are the ones who run the government. [1]

6. **Democracy is all about using the right to choose or vote. A democratic government is dependent on people's viewpoint. A leader is only able to win the democratic country, if he or she has given the valued people's opinion and make them top priority. However doing this is not enough. Once the leader has been chosen by the people, right from the next day citizens start evaluating their deeds and the process becomes very transparent. So transparency is the main factor of a democratic government by which a leader needs to be very responsive to the needs and expectation of the citizens.** [1 + 1 + 1]

7. **In a democratic country, majority and minority should work together. It should be the duty of government that both the groups respect each other's cultures. Needs and aspirations of every section of society should be looked by a democratic country. There should be equal participation of the citizen in government policies. The government should be able to solve conflicts between two communities without any discrimination. For example, in Belgium, the government negotiated the differences between two linguistic communities.** [1 + 1 + 1]

8. **"Democracy is seen to be good in principle but felt to be not so good in practice". The reasons for this are:**

   (i) In a democracy, people expect to have their needs fulfilled but it is not possible to look after everyone's needs as every country has diverse culture and regions. This often frustrates the common people. [1]

(ii) Ideally in a democracy everyone should be treated equally but there are instances where the minority opinion is not taken into account for a general view. [1]

(iii) Democracy is a people's government and it is imperative that people cast their vote to choose a government. But, many people skip the voting which does not serve the purpose of democracy. [1]

(iv) Regular elections may lead to change in ruling party and every party works in a different way. This may cause instability. [1]

(v) The people as well as the country will suffer if people are not wise enough in choosing a decent representative. [1]

9. **In today's society, every individual expects to get proper respect. Democracy stands for every individual's freedom and respect. Democracy gives the power to each individual, so s/he can fight back for their dignity.** [1 + 1]

   Still, there are societies which have been built for long on the basis of subordination and domination. it is not a simple thing to accept that all individual are equal. [1]

   If we talk about the respect of women, it's been ages that most of the societies are male dominated. Women struggled for long to get their respect and dignity. They also need to be treated equally and for such a situation Democracy comes forward and stands to promote dignity. [1 + 1]

10. **Democracy leads to peaceful and harmonious life among citizens –**

   (i) Democracy accommodates various social divisions. [1]

(ii) Democracy reduces the possibility of tensions becoming explosive and violent. [1]

(iii) Ability to handle social differences and conflicts among different groups is a plus point of democracy. [1]

(iv) Democracy develops procedure to conduct healthy competitions among different groups in a society. [1]

(v) Democracy respects differences and provides mechanism to resolve them. [1]

(vi) Democracy always accommodates minority view.

MULTIPLE CHOICE QUESTIONS

1. Democracies have not helped in removing:
   - (*a*) Economic inequalities
   - (*b*) Infrastructural problems
   - (*c*) Political conflicts
   - (*d*) All of the above

2. Democracies are based on political equality as:
   - (*a*) It assures employment for all
   - (*b*) It establishes constitutional monarchy
   - (*c*) It grants every individual the right to vote
   - (*d*) None of these

3. What is meant by an accountable government?
   - (*a*) In an accountable government, people have the right to elect the leaders to form government and if possible they participate in decision-making process
   - (*b*) In an accountable government, people do not have the right to elect the leaders.
   - (*c*) In an accountable government, people are not a part of decision-making process.
   - (*d*) In an accountable government, only under privileged section of the society are allowed to vote

4. A legally chosen government is called as......
   - (*a*) Dictatorship
   - (*b*) Legitimate government
   - (*c*) Monarchy
   - (*d*) None of these

5. Non – democratic regimes suppress ......
   - (*a*) External social differences
   - (*b*) Internal economic differences
   - (*c*) External gender differences
   - (*d*) Internal social differences

Answer Keys

1. (*a*)
2. (*c*)
3. (*a*)
4. (*b*)
5. (*d*)

FILL IN THE BLANKS

1. A democratic government provides .... for arriving at a decision.
2. Increase in domestic production and services leading to an all – round growth in people's standard of living are known as________________.
3. Democracy is based on the idea of____________ and negotiation.
4. In Bangladesh, more than half of its population lives in ______________.
5. Accommodating the demands of ___________ communities reduces the possibility of problems

Solutions

1. Rules and procedures
2. Economic growth
3. Deliberation
4. Poverty
5. Minority

TRUE OR FALSE

1. Democratic form of government is considered as the best.
2. Unequal distribution of income and opportunity between different groups in society is called as gender inequality.
3. Democracy provides an opportunity for rectifying errors.
4. Dictatorships have higher rate of economic growth..
5. Every society can fully and permanently resolve conflicts among different groups..

Solutions

1. True
2. False
3. True
4. True
5. False

Unit IV : Economics

CHAPTER 1

Money and Credit

Summary

Money and Credit

- Money is a medium of exchange.
- Money includes currency paper notes and coin.
- Money is in the form of currency authorized by the government as medium of exchange.
- In India the Reserve bank of India issues currency on behalf of the Central Government.

Banks

- People deposit their extra cash in banks by opening accounts in their names.
- Banks accept the deposits and also pay an amount as interest on deposits.
- As cash Banks keeps only a small share of their deposits as per RBI guidelines.
- Bank charges money on providing facilities.
- Bank mediates between depositors and borrowers.

Credit terms and types

Term of credit

- Collateral
- Interest rate
- Documentation
- Mode of repayment

Type

Formal sector

- Formal sector loan is given by commercial banks.
- Collateral is required in this sector.

- It has a low rate of interest on loan.
- It is controlled or supervised by Reserve Bank of India.

Informal sector

- The loan taken from friends, moneylenders, and relatives is termed as informal sector loan.
- Interest is not fixed, it is usually higher than formal.
- There is no supervisory body for this sector.
- Collateral is not required in most cases
- It often creates a situation of debt trap.

Points to know

Double coincidence of wants

What a person desires to sell is exactly what the other wishes to buy

Cheque

A cheque is a paper instructing the bank to pay a specific amount to the person, in whose name the cheque has been issued.

Collateral

An asset of borrower that is used as a guarantee to obtain a loan from lender.

SHG

A self-help group (SHG) is a village-based financial intermediary committee usually composed of 10–200 local women or men. They are exclusive groups started primarily to empower women in rural and suburban areas, make them economically independent and help them contribute to the socio-economic development of the nation.

PREVIOUS YEARS'
EXAMINATION QUESTIONS

▶ 1 Mark Questions

1. Which one of the following is not a feature of money?
   (*a*) Medium of exchange
   (*b*) Lack of divisibility
   (*c*) A store of value
   (*d*) A unit of account
   [TERM 2, 2011]

2. Professor Muhammad Yunus is the founder of which one of the following banks?
   (*a*) Co-operative Bank
   (*b*) Commercial Bank
   (*c*) Grameen Bank
   (*d*) Land Development Bank
   [TERM 2, 2011]

3. Which one of the following statements is most appropriate regarding transactions made in money?
   (*a*) It is the easiest way
   (*b*) It is the safest way
   (*c*) It is the cheapest way
   (*d*) It promotes trade
   [TERM 2, 2012]

4. Which of the following is the main informal source of credit for rural household in India?
   (*a*) Friends
   (*b*) Relatives
   (*c*) Landlords
   (*d*) Money Lenders
   [TERM 2, 2013]

5. What is meant by double coincidence of wants?
   [TERM 2, 2015]

6. How does money act as a medium of exchange?
   [TERM 2, 2015]

7. Why are most of the poor households deprived from the formal sector of loans?
   [TERM 2, 2016]

8. Give any two examples of informal sector of credit.
   [DELHI, 2018]

▶ 3 Marks Questions

9. What is money? Why is modern money currency accepted as a medium of exchange?
   [TERM 2, 2012, 2013]

10. Why is cheap and affordable credit important for the country's development? Explain three reasons.
    [TERM 2, 2012]

11. Why is modern currency accepted as a medium of exchange without any use of its own? Find out the reason.
    [TERM 2, 2015]

12. Explain any three loan activities of banks in India.
    [TERM 2, 2017]

▶ 4 Marks Questions

13. Explain any four terms of credit with examples.
    [TERM 2, 2011]

▶ 5 Marks Questions

14. How do banks play an important role in the economy of India? Explain.
    [TERM 2, 2015]

15. How can the formal sector loans be made beneficial for poor farmers and workers? Suggest any five measures.
    [TERM 2, 2017]

🔑 Solutions

1. Lack of divisibility [1]
2. Grameen Bank [1]
3. It promotes trade [1]
4. (*d*) Money Lenders [1]
5. Double coincidence of wants mean, if a person desires to sell what exactly other person wishes to buy. Goods are directly exchanged without the use of the money in this coincidence. [1]
6. For all the sellers, money acts as a medium of exchange for the goods they sell. A seller has to find a buyer for his goods, who can pay a good amount in the reversal of goods seller sells. When money acts as a medium of exchange, the need for double coincidence of want eliminates as the person only find the buyer for their goods. [1]
7. Most of the poor households are deprived from the formal sector of loans because:
   (*i*) In rural India formal banks are not present everywhere. [0.5]
   (*ii*) Absence of collateral and properdocument. [0.5]

(*iii*) Moneylenders charge very high rates of interest keeping no records of the transactions and then they harass the poor borrowers but they preferred to take loan from moneylenders as no paper work or other formalities are needed in it

8. (*i*) Moneylenders   [0.5]

   (*ii*) Traders   [0.5]

   (*iii*) Employers

   (*iv*) Relatives or friends

9. Something that acts as a medium of exchange in transactions of goods and services can be taken as Money. It also serves as a standard unit to determine their value.   [1]

   The government of the country has authorized the currency therefore modern money currency is accepted as a medium of exchange for easier transactions and promotion of trade.   [1]

   Example:

   Indian rupee is widely accepted as a medium of exchange in India. The rupee currency notes issued on behalf of Indian government by the Reserve Bank of India, cannot be refused by anybody. They have to accept rupees in exchange of goods and services in India.   [1]

10. Cheap and affordable credit is important for the country's development because:

    (*i*) The more lending, the higher the incomes and that encourages people to invest in agriculture, engage in business and set up small scale industries.   [1]

    (*ii*) Affordable can end the cycle of debt trap and lead to sustainable economic activity that allows borrowers to invest in better technology to make their business more competitive.   [1]

    (*iii*) Cheap credit would also allow weaker sections of society to enter formal sector of lending and rid them of exploitation at the hands of informal moneylenders.   [1]

11. Modern currency is accepted as a medium of exchange despite having no use of its own because the currency is authorized by the government of the country. The currency is issued by Reserve bank of India on the behalf of central government. This bank has all rights reserved to issue the currency and no other organisation is allowed to issue the currency. The law has permitted the use of rupee as a medium of payment that cannot be refused in making any transaction in India.   [1 + 1 + 1]

12. Following are the loan activities of banks in India:

    (*i*) For economic activities, loans are provided by the bank.   [1]

    (*ii*) Bank offers less interest on deposit but charges more interest on loans.   [1]

    (*iii*) A small proportion of deposit is kept by the bank as cash to provide a loan. It acts as an intermediate between those who have a fund (deposit) and those who need that fund.   [1]

13. The terms of credit basically comprises of Interest rate, Collateral and documentation requirement, and the mode of repayment.

    (*i*) Interest rate: The amount due for a particular period of time on the amount lent, deposited or borrowed is known as Interest rate. This is paid by the borrower to the lender along with the principal amount.
                                                [1]

    (*ii*) Collateral: Collateral is an asset that the borrower owns and uses this as a guarantee to a lender until the loan is repaid.   [1]

    (*iii*) Documentation: Documentation required by the lender before lending money includes identification of the borrower such as the employment records or salary slips.
                                                [1]

    (*iv*) Mode of Repayment: This defines the way or the duration on the basis of which the borrower will return back the money to the lender.   [1]

14. (*i*) Banks provide credit at cheap and affordable rates to the poor.   [1]

    (*ii*) Banks accept the deposits and also pay an amount as interest on the deposits.   [1]

    (*iii*) Banks use a major portion of the deposits to give loans.   [1]

    (*iv*) Banks helps in establishment of large scale industries which brings foreign exchange, and thus adds to the national income of the country.   [1]

    (*v*) Provides employment and growth opportunities to the low income groups.
                                                [1]

    Above all, banks ensure the flow of liquidity in market and help to generate capital by various means.

15. Below are the five measures to make the formal sector loans beneficial for poor farmers and workers.

(i) Unlike the informal lenders, formal sector loans should charge less interest on loans. [1]

(ii) Number of banks should increase in rural areas, so services can reach most of the poor people. [1]

(iii) There should be an availability of information and help counter in each bank, so a person can get information regarding the loan properly. [1]

(iv) More and more people should be encouraged to take loan from formal sectors instead of going to other sectors. [1]

(v) It should be checked that each person is getting right amount as a loan and their transaction should be checked properly. [1]

MULTIPLE CHOICE QUESTIONS

1. Which of these is an advantage of money?
   (a) It is available to everyone
   (b) It can be used as for direct exchange of goods
   (c) It eliminates the need for double coincidence of wants
   (d) Both (b) and (c)

2. Who has the authority to issue currency in India?
   (a) RBI- Reserve Bank of India
   (b) SBI- State Bank of India
   (c) TATA
   (d) BHEL

3. Which of these is a modern form of money?
   (a) Silver coins
   (b) Exchange of food
   (c) Renting property
   (d) Paper currency

4. Which of these is a source of credit?
   (a) Banks
   (b) Parents
   (c) Teachers
   (d) Neighbors

5. What is Collateral?
   (a) It is a gift provided by a borrower (such as land, building, vehicle, livestock, deposits with banks) against a loan, and it can be sold in case of non-payment of loan.
   (b) It is the security provided by a borrower (such as land, building, vehicle, livestock, deposits with banks) against a loan, and it can be sold in case of non-payment of loan.
   (c) It is a promise provided by a borrower
   (d) Both (a) and (c)

Answer Keys

1. (c)   2. (a)   3. (d)   4. (a)   5. (b)

FILL IN THE BLANKS

1. A ____________ is a written instruction to a bank by an account holder to pay a specific sum to a specific person from his deposit.

2. Farmers require credit to purchase ____________.

3. Banks use only a small portion of the ____________ to extend loans.

4. ____________ and ____________ are sources of formal sector loans.

5. Payments which are to be made in the future are known as____________.

Solutions

1. Cheque
2. The raw materials and inputs for agriculture
3. Deposits
4. Banks, Cooperatives
5. Deferred Payments

TRUE OR FALSE

1. Banks play an important role in developing the economy of India.

2. A loan is usually given for a specific duration of time and needs to be completely repaid by a specified date.

3. Informal lenders charge low rate of interest.

4. Before the introduction of coins, a variety of objects were used as money.

5. Deposits with the banks are not beneficial to the depositors or to the nation.

Solutions

1. True
2. True
3. False
4. True
5. False

Globalisation and The Indian Economy

Summary
Globalisation

- Globalisation is the process of sharing ideas, goods and services, culture between countries by the help of various means.
- Globalisation paced due to development in transportation and communication technology.
- The economic interactions enabled Globalisation, which also help in the intermingle of social and cultural aspects.
- Globalisation enables the production of goods and services, globally.
- MNCs divide the production of goods and services in small parts and spread out across the globe.
- MNCs setup production jointly with local companies.
- Joint production provides money for additional investment and latest technology for production.
- MNC's generally, work with local companies as a partner, sometimes they buys local companies. In both condition, MNC's use the market setup by the local companies.

Foreign trade and integration of the market

- Foreign trade was the main channel of connecting countries.
- Exchange of goods, across the geographical boundaries of countries.
- Creates an opportunity for the producers to reach beyond the domestic markets or their countries' market.
- Goods travel from one market to another.
- In the market, choice of goods go up.
- Price of similar goods in two markets tend to be equal.
- Producers of two companies closely compete against each other even if they are distant. In this way foreign trade connects markets.

Challenges and Factors that enabled Globalisation

- Rapid improvement in technology is a major factor which paced the Globalisation process.
- Technological change, especially in communications technology. Internet enables us to send instant electronic mail and talk across the world at negligible costs.
- Free Trade. Many barriers to trade have been removed. Some of this has been done by regional groupings of countries such as the EU. Most of it has been done by the WTO. This makes trade cheaper and therefore more attractive to business.

Challenges

- To make globalization beneficial for developing countries.
- To ensure the sharing of benefits among all countries.
- To ensure the proper and strict functioning of the organization involving in trade rules .
- To ensure the minimization of growing disparities between rich and poor.

- To ensure the development of small scale industries.
- To ensure the safeguarding of workers

Globalisation and its impact

- Greater competition among producers both local and foreign producers has been of advantage to producers.
- Greater choice for consumers of improved quality and lower price of products.
- Living standard of people is changing to higher standards.
- Foreign investments have increased.
- New jobs have been created.
- Increased competition has encouraged top Indian companies to invest in newer technology and production methods and raise their production quality.
- Globalisation has enabled some large companies to emerge as multinational companies.
- Creates new opportunities for companies providing services particularly those involving Information Technology

Points to know

MNCs

Multinational companies like Nestle, Cargil foods, Reebook etc

Trade Barrier

Tax on import or export to control foreign trade.

Liberalisation

Removal of barriers from trade set by the government.

SEZs

Special economic zone is set up by the government to attract foreign companies to invest in India by providing infrastructure and giving five year tax waive off in the initial period.

PREVIOUS YEARS' EXAMINATION QUESTIONS

▷ 1 Mark Questions

1. Which of the following is not a feature of a Multi-National Company?
   (a) It owns/controls production in more than one nation.
   (b) Its sets up factories where it is close to the markets.
   (c) It organizes production in complex ways.
   (d) It employs labour only from its own country.
   [TERM 2, 2011]

2. 'Cargill Foods' is the largest producer of which of the following in India?
   (a) Medicines
   (b) Asian Paints
   (c) Edible oil
   (d) Garments
   [TERM 2, 2012]

3. Which of the following is a 'barrier' on foreign trade?
   (a) Tax on import
   (b) Quality Control
   (c) Sales Tax
   (d) Tax on local trade
   [TERM 2, 2013]

4. Why do MNCs set up their offices and factories in those regions where they get cheap labour and other resources?
   [TERM 2, 2014]

▷ 3 Marks Questions

5. Explain any three advantages of globalization.
   [TERM 2, 2011]

6. What is a trade barrier? Why did the Indian Government put up trade barriers after Independence? Explain.
   [TERM 2, 2011]

7. How are M.N.Cs. spreading their production across countries? Explain with an example.
   [TERM 2, 2012]

8. What would happen if Government of India puts heavy tax on import of Chinese toys? Explain any three points.
   [TERM 2, 2012]

9. How do Multi-National Companies manage to keep the cost of production of their goods low? Explain with examples.
   [TERM 2, 2013]

10. "Foreign trade integrated the markets in different countries." Support the statement with arguments.
    [TERM 2, 2015]

11. How do Multi-National Corporations (MNCs) interlink production across countries? Explain with examples.
    [TERM 2, 2017]

▷ 5 Marks Questions

12. How have our markets been transformed in recent years? Explain with examples.
    [TERM 2, 2013]

13. "Globalization has been advantageous to consumers as well as to producers." Support the statement with suitable examples.

[TERM 2, 2014]

14. "Globalization and greater competition among producers has been advantageous to consumers." Support the statement with examples.

[TERM 2, 2015]

15. Describe the impact of globalization on Indian economy with examples.

[TERM 2, 2016]

16. Analyze any five positive effects of Globalization on the Indian economy.

[TERM 2, 2017]

17. What is liberalization? Describe any four effects of liberalisation on the Indian economy.

[TERM 2, 2017]

18. How do we feel the impact of globalization on our daily life? Explain with examples.

[DELHI 2018]

Solutions

1. (d) It employs labour only from its own country. [1]

2. (c) Edible oil [1]

3. (a) Tax on import [1]

4. MNCs set up their offices and factories in those regions where they get cheap labour and other resources to save costs and increase profit. [1]

5. Globalization is the process or trend of increasing interaction between people or companies on a world wide scale with the help of various means

(i) It helped many large companies in India to turn into MNCs which are spreading their operations worldwide. Globalization has also created new opportunities for various sectors like IT. [1]

(ii) There is a greater choice before the consumers who now enjoy products with improved quality at lower prices. [1]

(iii) Globalization also broadened minds. It has led to the flow of ideas across national boundaries. [1]

6. Trade Barrier is a kind of restriction that has been set up on the foreign trade and foreign investment by the Indian government. Quotas and taxes on imports are used to regulate trade. Tax on imports is an example of trade barrier. It can be used to regulate foreign trade and decide what and how much should come into the country. [1 + 1]

After Independence, the Indian Government had to put the trade barriers on the foreign trade and investment. This was emphasized at that time so as to get rid of the foreign competition. During 1950s and 1960s, Inian industries were coming it up and foreign competition at that stage won't allow them to settle. Thus, India allowed imports of only essential items such as machinery, fertilizers, petroleum, etc. [1]

7. MNCs spread their production across countries through the following ways:

(i) MNCs set up offices and factories for production in regions where they can get cheap labour and other resources. [1]

(ii) MNCs set up production jointly with some of the local companies of these countries. [1]

(iii) MNCs make capital and technology investments and buy up local companies and then expand production.

For example: Cargill Foods, a very large American MNC, has bought over smaller Indian companies such as Parakh Foods. Parakh Foods had built a large marketing network in various parts of India, where its brand was well-reputed. Also, Parakh Foods had four oil refineries, whose control has now shifted to Cargill. Cargill is now the largest producer of edible oil in India. [1]

8. If the Government of India puts heavy tax on import of Chinese toys the following situations would likely occur:

(i) The Chinese toys would become costly to the Indian customers and the imports from China would reduce. [1]

(ii) The domestic toy making companies will have more opportunities to capture the larger share of domestic market. [1]

(iii) The Chinese government would also bring up the trade barriers. [1]

9. A company that owns or controls production in more than one country is known as Multi-National Company (MNC).

Multi-National companies manage to keep cost of production of their goods low by:

(i) Setting up offices and factories for production in countries or places where cheap labor is easily available. USA companies outsourcing production to china. [1]

(ii) Setting up trade and distribution centers in region close to their markets or stores. [1]

(*iii*) Setting up production in area where raw material or other resources are available at low cost with an objective to earn higher profits. [1]

10. Foreign trade is all about expanding the business beyond the domestic market. Many foreign traders expand their business in other countries too, e.g. Initially toys were quite expensive in India which was not affordable for every household. China took this as an advantage and brought toys in cheap prices and with different varieties people liked their products and China got a good response from Indian market where as Indian toy sellers get opposite response. So with the opening trade goods travel from one market to another. Choice of goods in the market rises and producers of two different countries get competent. Foreign trade thus results in connecting the markets. [1 + 1 + 1]

11. (*i*) MNCs buy local small companies to sell their products in large areas of the country. For example- Cargill foods bought Parakh, a smaller Indian company having a large marketing network in various part of India and became the largest producer of edible oil. [1]

(*ii*) Small industries produce raw material for these Multi-National Corporations which helps them to grow as well. [1]

(*iii*) Sometimes, money for advance investments for setting up new machines are provided by MNCs to increase the production. [1]

12. Our markets have been transformed in recent years in the following ways:

(*i*) The economy of our country has grown rapidly with the onset of LPG (Liberalisation, Privatisation and Globalisation) reforms in 1991. [1]

(*ii*) Earlier the production was specified to a particular place. In recent years, production is widely dispersed at several locations with interlinked communication. [1]

(*iii*) Foreign trade has increased rapidly, connecting and integrating the markets in different countries. [1]

(*iv*) In the recent years, technology in the areas of telecommunication, computers and internet has developed exponentially. Due to this, many companies have evolved providing services in the field of IT. [1]

(*v*) Globalization has enabled some large Indian companies like Tata Motors (auto-mobiles), Infosys (IT), Ranbaxy (medicine) to emerge as multi-national companies. [1]

13. Globalization has been advantageous to producers as-

(*i*) With investment in newer technology and production methods, producers have raised their production standards which have enabled them to produce good quality products and make them available in the international markets. This paves the way to boost exports. [1]

(*ii*) As the markets expand, the producers now have a large number of well-off buyers. [1]

(*iii*) Globalization has helped some large domestic companies to emerge as multinationals themselves. Ex. Tata Motors and Ranbaxy. [1]

Globalization has been advantageous to consumers as-

(*i*) The consumers can choose from a large and different variety of products with improved quality and lower prices. [1]

(*ii*) Since Globalization paves a way for international markets, people today enjoy much higher standard of living than was possible earlier. [1]

(*iii*) Globalization has led to the creation of new jobs.

14. Advantages of globalization to customers can be described in the following ways:

(*i*) The increased competition has led producers to provide products at comparatively cheaper rates. [1]

(*ii*) Consumers now have the option to select from a variety of products. [1]

(*iii*) It has increased capital flows, and comparatively greater amount of trade which helps the consumer to fulfill their development goals. [1]

(*iv*) It has played a vital role in generation of employment and an increase in movement of labour from one country to another by which opportunity and scope of employment increased. [1]

(*v*) Globalization promotes spread of innovative ideas and technology. [1]

(*vi*) It increases dependency of one country on another as a means of trade which contributes to world peace.

15. Globalization of the Indian economy has come a long way. MNCs have increased in India over the past 20 years, which means investing in India has been beneficial for them. [1]

They are expanding in different industries such as cell phones, automobiles, electronics, soft drinks, fast food or services such as banking in urban areas. [1]

Globalization has mostly had a good impact on Indian economy. Some Indian companies emerged as multidimensional themselves! E.g. Tata Motors, Infosys, Ranbaxy, Asian Paints etc. Because of the expansion of these companies chances of employment have increased on an exponential rate. [1 + 1]

Globalization has increased the opportunity of employment ,which paced the service sector in India . It helped in the upliftment of living standard of our citizens by providing wide range of goods and services at affordable prices. [1]

16. Following are the positive effects of globalization on the Indian economy:

(*i*) Foreign investment has increased over the past years. [1]

(*ii*) New opportunities are created by globalization for Indian companies especially those providing services like IT. [1]

(*iii*) Globalization has increased competition and it is beneficial for some of the top companies like Tata Motors and Infosys because it made them able to get benefit from this increased competition. [1]

(*iv*) The rate of unemployment has been reduced to an extent because because new job opportunities are created due to of globalization. [1]

(*v*) Services which were costly such as data entry, accounting, administrative tasks, and engineering now became cheap in India.[1]

17. Liberalization means the opening of the country for foreign investments and capitals. Countries use trade barriers to protect the domestic industries from foreign products. To protect local markets, countries resort to impose licenses, import quotas or voluntary export restraints.
[1]

Following are the impacts of liberalization on the Indian economy:

(*i*) Foreign trade has increased. [1]

(*ii*) Foreign investment has increased. [1]

(*iii*) Countries are exchanging technologies that help in modernization of India. [1]

(*iv*) Better job opportunities are created, which solve the problem of unemployment. [1]

18. Impact of Globalization-

(*i*) Globalization and greater competition among producers has been beneficial to consumers. [1]

(*ii*) Greater choice before consumers like lexcury automobiles. [1]

(*iii*) Availability of standard quality products at lower price. [1]

(*iv*) Foreign investments have increased in many areas like cell phones, auto mobiles, electronics, soft drinks etc. [1]

(*v*) New job, have been created. [1]

(*vi*) Several Indian manufacturing units have shut down rendering many workers jobless.

MULTIPLE CHOICE QUESTIONS

1. Which authority in India has laid emphasis on the development of foreign trade in the five year plans?

(*a*) Election Commission

(*b*) Human Rights Commission

(*c*) Planning Commission

(*d*) All of the above

2. Which of these has been one major factor that has stimulated the globalisation process?

(*a*) Rapid improvement in information and communication technology

(*b*) People's fondness of moving abroad

(*c*) People's curiosity about foreign products

(*d*) Government policies

3. Where do MNCs setup their production units?

(*a*) At a place where they can produce their goods at a minimum cost

(*b*) Close to nature

(*c*) At a place where food is available in abundance

(*d*) At a place where water is available in abundance

4. What is the process of buying and selling goods and services between two or more than two countries is known as?

    (*a*) Foreign investment (*b*) Banking

    (*c*) Foreign Trade   (*d*) None of these

5. Which of these indicate that markets have been transformed in recent years?

    (*a*) Everyone goes to a shopping mall

    (*b*) We have a wide choice of goods and services before us

    (*c*) People do only online shopping

    (*d*) Prices of all goods have reduced significantly

Answer Keys

   1. (*c*)   2. (*a*)   3. (*a*)   4. (*c*)   5. (*b*)

FILL IN THE BLANKS

1. Globalisation and greater competition among producers has been advantageous to____________.

2. ____________________ of an economy means to free it from direct or physical controls imposed by the government.

3. A tax or duty to be paid on a particular class of imports or exports is called as ___________.

4. MNCs are setting up their customer care centers in India due to availability of _________ labour.

5. Government has allowed _____________ in the labour laws to attract foreign investment.

Solutions

1. Consumers
2. Liberalisation
3. Tariff
4. Cheap
5. Flexibility

TRUE OR FALSE

1. The impact of globalisation has not been uniform.

2. Tata Motors is an foreign MNC.

3. WTO rules have forced the developing contries to remove trade barriers.

4. The Indian Government had lifted barriers on foreign trade and foreign investment after Independence

5. The idea behind the development of Special Economic Zones (SEZs) in India is to attract foreign investment

Solutions

1. True
2. False
3. True
4. False
5. True

CBSE
Solved Paper 2019

Social Science
Class X

Time : 3 hrs   MM : 80

General Instructions

(i) The question paper is divided into four sections – Section A, Section B, Section C and Section D.

(ii) The question paper has 26 questions in all.

(iii) All questions are compulsory.

(iv) Marks are indicated against each question.

(v) Questions from serial number 1 to 7 are very short answer type questions. Each question carries one mark.

(vi) Questions from serial number 8 to 18 are 3 marks questions. Answer of these questions should not exceed 80 words each.

(vii) Questions from serial number 19 to 25 are 5 marks questions. Answers of these questions should not exceed 100 words each.

(viii) Question number 26 is a map question. It has 5 marks with two parts 26(A) and 26(B). 26(A) from History (2 marks) and 26(B) from Geography (3 marks). After completion attach the map inside your answer book.

SECTION A

1. How had hand printing technology introduced in Japan?   (1)

OR

How had translation process of novels into regional languages helped to spread their popularity?

2. Interpret the contribution of French in the economic development of Mekong delta region.   (1)

OR

Interpret the concept of 'liberalisation' in the field of economic sphere during the nineteenth century in Europe.

3. What may be a goal of landless rural labourers regarding their income?   (1)

OR

What may be a goal of prosperous farmer of Punjab.

4. How can democratic reforms be carried out by political parties? (1)

5. How is over–irrigation responsible for land degradation in Punjab? (1)

OR

How is cement industry responsible for land degradation?

6. Distinguish between 'primary' and secondary sectors. (1)

7. Explain the importance of formal sector loans in India. (1)

Section B

8. Describe any three main features of 'Rabi crop season'. (3)

OR

Describe any three main features of 'Kharif crop season'.

9. How had Napoleonic code exported to the regions under French control? Explain with examples. (3)

OR

Explain with examples three barriers that are responsible to economic growth in Vietnam.

10. How had the Imperial State in China been the major producer of printed material for a long time? Explain with examples (3)

OR

How had novels been easily available to the masses in Europe during nineteenth century? Explain with examples.

11. Analyse the impact of 'water scarcity'. (3)

12. "Consequences of environmental degradation do not respect national or state boundaries" Justify the statement (3)

13. Why is the 'tertiary sector' becoming important in India? Explain any three reasons. (3)

OR

How do we count various goods and services for calculating gross domestic product (G.D.P) of a country? Explain with example.

14. Explain any three functions of opposition political parties. (3)

15. How can consumers use their 'Right to seek redressal' Explain with example. (3)

16. "The assertion of social diversities in a democratic country is very normal and can be healthy" Justify the statement with arguments. (3)

OR

"Social divisions affect politics" Examine the statement.

17. "Women still lag much behind men in India despite some improvements since independence" Analyse the statement. (3)

18. Describe the importance of formal sources of credit in the economic development. (3)

OR

Describe the bad effects of informal sources of credit on borrowers.

SECTION C

19. "Roadways still have an edge over railways in India." Support the statement with example.

    $(5 \times 1 = 5)$

20. Compare the situation of Belgium and Sri Lanka considering their location, size and cultural aspects. $(1 + 1 + 3 = 5)$

    OR

    How is the idea of power sharing emerged? Explain different forms that have common arrangements of power sharing.

21. Explain five types of 'Industrial pollution'. (5)

22. Who had organized the Dalits into the 'Depressed classes Association' in 1930? Describe his achievements.

    OR (5)

    Define the term 'Civil Disobedience Movement'. Describe the participation of rich and poor peasant communities in the 'Civil Disobedience Movement'

23. "Indian trade had played a crucial role in the late nineteenth century world economy" Analyze the statement. $(5 \times 1 = 5)$

    OR

    "Series of changes affected the pattern of industrialization in India by the early twentieth century" Analyze the statement.

    OR

    "Industrialization had changed the form of urbanization in the modern period." Analyze the statement with special reference of London.

24. Describe any five factors that make democracy is a better form of government than other alternatives. $(5 \times 1 = 5)$

25. Explain any five facilities available in the special economic zones developed by the Central and State Governments to attract foreign investment. $(5 \times 1 = 5)$

SECTION D

26. (A) Two features A and B are marked on the given political outline map of India. Identify these features with the help of the following information and write their correct names on the lines marked near them. $(1 \times 3 = 3)$

    (a) The place where the Indian National Congress Session was held.

    (b) The city where Jallianwalla Bagh incident took place.

    (B) Locate and lanel any three of the following with appropriate symbols

    on the same given outline political map of India. $(1 \times 3 = 3)$

    (i) Kalpakkam   –   Nuclear Power Plant

    (ii) Vijayanagar   –   Iron and Steel Plant

    (iii) Noida   –   Software Technology Park

    (iv) Paradeep   –   Sea Port

    (v) Sardar Sarovar   –   Dam

Solution

SECTION A

1. Buddhist missionaries from China introduced hand-printing technology into Japan around AD 768-770. The oldest Japanese book, printed in AD 868, is the Buddhist 'Diamond Sutra'. Containing six sheets of text and woodcut illustrations. Pictures were printed on textiles, playing cards and paper money which made publishing very interesting. (1)

OR

English novels translated into regional Indian languages were initially not very popular as the Indian people could not relate the stories and characters to their own lives. But translation process of novels bring different spoken languages of people closer. These novels produce the sense of a shared world between diverse people in a nation. Novels also bring understanding of different cultures and values. (1)

2. The French began by building canals and draining lands in the Mekong delta to increase cultivation to bring about economic development. They used labour for construction of irrigation facilities to improve rice cultivation, built infrastructure and transportation facilities for the export of agricultural produce. (1)

OR

The term 'liberalism' is derived from the Latin word 'liber' means free. In the economic sphere. liberalism stood for the freedom of markets and the abolition of state–imposed restrictions on the movement of goods and capital. (1)

3. Development goals for, landless rural labourers regarding their income would be: (1)

    (i)   To get more days of work and better wages.

    (ii) To get quality education for their children.

    (iii) No social discrimination

OR

Development goals for prosperous farmers of Punjab would be (1)

    (i)   Low price of food grains.

    (ii) Assured high family income through higher support prices for their crops.

    (iii) Hardworking and cheap labourers.

4. Political parties need to have strong internal democracy, avoid dynastic succession, money and muscle power and by offering meaningful choice to the voters which could lead to democratic reforms. (1)

5. Water is very important for the growth of plant but excessive irrigation of field leads to water logging of soil. Therefore, over–irrigation is responsible for land degradation due to water–logging which leads to increase in salinity and alkalinity in the soil. (1)

OR

Excessive mining of limestone, silica and gypsum which are used as raw material for cement industry leads to land degradation. It later on settles down in the surrounding areas, affecting infiltration of water and crop cultivation. (1)

6. **Primary Sectors:** The primary sector is also called agriculture sector. It constitutes the backbone of our economy and the major sources of employment. Primary activity which is involved with the production or extraction of natural resources. (1/2)

   Secondary Sectors: Secondary sector involves use of natural goods and transform them into something more valuable by the manufacturing process. It is also called industrial sector. (1/2)

7. Importance of formal sector loans in India:

   (i)   The rate of interest charged on formal sector is lower than of informal sources of credit. (1/2)

   (ii) Reserve Bank of India supervises their function. (1/2)

Section B

8. There are three main features of 'Rabi crop reason'

   (i)   Rabi crops are grown in winter from October to December and harvested in summer from April to June. (1)

   (ii) Some Rabi crops are wheat, barley, peas, gram and mustard. (1)

   (iii) These crops are grown in large parts of India such as Punjab, Haryana and Himachal Pradesh etc. (1)

   OR

   There are three main features of 'Kharif crop season'

   (i)   Kharif crops are grown with the onset of monsoon and harvested in September–October. (1)

   (ii) Some important crops are paddy. maize, jowar, bajra, toor, moong, urad, cotton etc. (1)

   (iii) Rice is an important Kharif crop. Some important rice growing regions are Assam, West Bengal, Coastal region of Odisha, Andhra Pradesh, Tamilnadu etc. (1)

9. The civil code of 1804, known as the Napoleonic code.

   These codes were the revolutionary principles of administration and were exported to the regions under French control. (1)

   For example, in the Dutch Republic in Switzerland, Italy and Germany. Napoleon simplified administrative divisive, abolished the feudal system and freed peasants from serfdom and manorial dues. (1)

   Peasants, workers and new businessman enjoyed a new–found freedom. Businessmen and small–scale producers of goods in particular, began to realise that uniform laws, standardised weights and measures and a common national currency would facilitate the movement and exchange of goods and capital from one region to another. (1)

   OR

   According to an influential writer and policy–maker Paul Bernard, several barriers to economic growth in Vietnam such as:

   (i)   High population level in Vietnam proved to be and obstacle to economic growth. (1)

   (ii) Low agricultural productivity was another barrier that hindered the economic growth. (1)

   (iii) Excessive indebtedness among the peasants that did not promote economic growth in Vietnam. (1)

   (iv) The French colonialists did little to industrialise Vietnam and in the rural areas, landlordism spread and the standard of living declined. (1)

10. The earliest print technique developed in China. The imperial state in China was a large bureaucratic system, that sponsored the printing technique by the way of conducting examinations. China possessed a huge bureaucratic system which recruited its personnel through civil service examinations. Textbooks for this examination were printed in vast numbers under the sponsorship of the imperial state. (2)

From the sixteenth century. the number of examinations candidates went up and that increased the volume of print which node the Imperial state in China a major producer of printed material for a long time. (2)

OR

The Novel was one of the first mass–produced items to be sold in Europe. Novels created a sense of belonging on the basis of ones language. They dealt with the life of common people and they were cheap. Publishing markets helped in more sell and production of novels which was available to the masses in Europe during nineteenth century. (2)

Technological improvements in printing brought down the price of books and innovations in marketing led to expanded sale. In France, publishers found that they could make super profits by hiring out novels by the hour. (1)

11. Water is an essential resource for humans. Water scarcity is indeed the outcome of large and growing population. Humans require water for their various activities and more the number of people more the consumption. Water scarcity may lead to following impacts:

(i) Ground water level will decline. (1)

(ii) It may adversely affect water availability that shall impact agriculture and industry. (1)

(iii) Food grain production will be affected which may affect food security of the country. (1)

12. It is true that environmental degradation do not respect national or state boundaries. It has international and global affects because our future is linked together through common environmental and ecological system. Global warming, acid rain etc are the issues that cannot be tackled by one nation. It is a global concern. (2)

For example, if Indian Thermal power plants are causing massive air pollution, it affects our neighbouring countries like Pakistan, Bangladesh, Sri Lanka and others as well. Similarly, deforestation in Brazil has caused disturbance in rainfall pattern throughout South America. (1)

13. Importance of Tertiary Sector in India:

(i) In any country, several services such as hospitals, educational institutions, post and telegraph services, defence, transport, banks etc, are required. These can be considered as basic services. (1)

(ii) In development of agriculture and industry leads to the development of services such as transport, trade, storage etc. Greater the development of the primary and secondary sectors, more would be the demand for such services. (1)

(iii) With the increase in income levels, certain sections of people start demanding many more services like tourism better educational facilities, communication services etc thereby, giving a boost to the tertiary sector. (1)

OR

The various goods and services are counted on the basis of the value of each goods or services, not on the basis of actual numbers.

(i) The value of final goods and services produced in each sector during a particular year provides the total production of the sector for that year. The sum of all the three sector's production within a country is known as Gross Domestic Product (G.D.P) of a country. (1½)

(ii) For example, a farmer sells wheat to a flour mill for ₹ 18/kg. The mill grinds the wheat and sells the flour to a biscuit company for ₹ 20/ kg. The biscuit company uses flour, sugar and oil to make the packets of biscuits. It sells biscuits in the market ₹ 45/ packet. Now, biscuits are the final goods. So, only the value of all final goods and services produced within a country during a particular year is counted as GDP. (1½)

14. Those parties that lose in the elections play the role of opposition to the parties in power. There are three functions of opposition political parties:

   (i) By voicing different views and criticizing government for its failures of programmes and wrong policies and their implementation. (1)

   (ii) It keeps people aware of wrong policies and programmes of the government. (1)

   (iii) It provides alternatives to choose from as it voices those views which are different from the party in power and helpful for the peoples of that country. (1)

15. **Right to Seek Redressal :** Consumers have the right to seek redressal against unfair trade practices and exploitation. If any damage is done to a consumer, he or she has the right to get a compensation depending on the degree of damage. There is a need to provide an easy and effective public system by which this can be done. (2)

   For example, Deepak had sent a money order to his village for his daughter's marriage. The money did not reach to his daughter at the time when she needed it nor did it reach month's later. Therefore, Deepak can filed a case in the district level consumer court and exercised right to seek redressal. (1)

16. Social diversities in a democratic country is very normal and healthy. It divides similar people from one another but also unite very different people belonging to different social groups. (1)

   The assertion of social diversities in a country does not require to be seen as a source of danger.

   (i) In a democracy, political expression of social divisions is very normal and can be healthy. This allows different disadvantaged and marginal social groups to express their grievances and get the government to attend these. (1)

   (ii) This leads to strengthening of a democracy. People who feel marginalized, deprived and discriminated, have to fight against the injustices. Such a fight often takes the democratic path, voicing their demands in a peaceful and constitutional manner and seeking a fair position through elections. (1)

OR

   All social differences and diversities do not lead to social divisions. A combination of social divisions and politics can be really dangerous. A democracy involves competition among various political parties. The cases of Sri Lanka and Yugoslavia are clear examples.

   While political competition along religious and ethnic lines led to the disintegration of Yugoslavia into six independent countries, the situation in Sri Lanka is also very explosive. Social divisions between the Sinhalese and Tamils are affecting politics of the country and have brought it in a civil war situation. (2)

   In a democracy, political parties would talk to these divisions, ask for votes on this basis, make different promises to the people and talk of politics to redress the grievances of the disadvantaged communities. (1)

17. Women still lag much behind men in India despite some improvements since independence. There are some factors to analyse the given statement:

   (i) Literacy Rate : The literacy rate among women is only 64.6% compared with 80.9% among men. A smaller proportion of girls go for higher studies.

   (ii) Low Sex – Ratio : Parents in India prefer to have sons. They also find ways to abort the girl child before she is born. Such sex–selective abortion has resulted in a decline in female child sex–ratio.

   (iii) Political Representation : In India, women representation in legislature has been very low, while in America, England etc, women are given seats in Parliament even though there are male members.

18. Formal sources of credit are beneficial in the sense that they provide credit at reasonable rates without any undue exploitative practices as faced under informal sources of credit. Importance of formal source of credit:

(i) The formal source of credit includes loan from banks and co–operatives. (½)

(ii) RBI supervises the functioning of formal sources of loans. (½)

(iii) RBI ensures that loans are given not only to the profit – making business man and traderss but also to small–cultivators, small–scale industries, small borrowers etc. (½)

(iv) Banks and co–operative societies need to lend more. This would lead to higher incomes and many people could then borrow cheaply for a variety of needs. They could grow crops, do business, set up small–industries etc. (½)

(v) Cheap and affordable credit by the formal sector is crucial for the country's development. (½)

OR

Informal sources of credit are the moneylenders, traders, employers, relatives and friends. There are some bad effects of informal sources of credit:

(i) The borrowers tend to find themselves in a debt–trap (½)

(ii) The rate of interest can be really high as it depends on the wishes of the lender. (½)

(iii) There is no organization to supervise its lending activities. (½)

(iv) The cost to the borrower becomes much higher that leads to less incomes. (½)

Section C

19. In India, roadways have preceded railways. They still have an edge over railways in view of the ease with which they can be built and maintained. The growing importance of road transport vis–a–vis rail transport is rooted in the following reasons:

(i) Construction cost of roads is much lower than that of railways lines. (1)

(ii) Roads can traverse comparatively more dissected and undulating topography. (1)

(iii) Roads can negotiate higher gradients of slopes and as such can traverse mountains such as the Himalayas. (1)

(iv) Road ways tend to provide door to door service, therefore the cost of loading and unloading is much lower. (1)

(v) Road transport is economical in transportation of few persons and small amount of goods over short distances. (1)

20. Belgium is a small country in Europe while Sri Lanka is an island nation is Asia. In Sri Lanka and Belgium, there were ethnic conflicts for power on the basis of the language. (1)

Belgium has a population of a little over one crore, about half the population of Haryana. whereas Sri Lanka has about two crore people, about the same as in Haryana. (1)

People of Belgium practice Christianity while people of Sri Lanka follow Buddhism. Out of Belgium's total population. 59% lives in Flemish region and speaks Dutch language and another 40% lives in Wallonia region and speak French while Sri Lankan social groups are Sinhala – speakers and Tamil speakers.

In Belgium, the Dutch community has advantage of its numeric majority and could forced its will on the French and German speaking population. In Sri Lanka, the Sinhala community enjoyed an even bigger majority and could imposed its will on the entire country. (3)

OR

It is true that the idea of power sharing emerged in opposition to the notions of undivided political power. In modern democracies, power sharing arrangements can take many forms.

Power is shared among different organs of government such as legislature, executive and Judiciary Power can be shared among governments at different levels. A general government for the entire country and governments at the provincial or regional level. (2)

Power may also be shared among different social groups such as the religious and linguistic groups. 'Community government' in Belgium is a good example of this arrangement.

Power sharing arrangements can also be seen in the way political parties, pressure groups and movements control or influence those in power. In a democracy, the citizens must have freedom to choose among various contenders for power. (3)

21. Although industries contributes significantly to India's economic growth and development, the increase in pollution of land, water, air, noise and resulting degradation of environment that they have caused cannot be overlooked.

(i) Air Pollution : It is caused by the presence of high proportion of undesirable gases, such as sulphur dioxide and carbon monoxide. Air–borne particulate materials contain both solid and liquid particles like dust, sprays mist and smoke. (1)

(ii) Water Pollution : It is caused by organic and inorganic industrial wastes and affluents discharged into rivers. The main culprits in this regard are paper, pulp, chemical textile and dyeing, petroleum refineries, tanneries and electroplating industries that let out dyes, detergents, acids, salts and heavy metals like lead and mercury pesticides (1)

(iii) Thermal Pollution : Thermal pollution of water occurs when hot water from factories and thermal plants is drained into rivers and ponds before cooling. (1)

(iv) Noise Pollution : Noise pollution not only results in hearing impairment, increased heart rate and blood pressure among other physiological effects. (1)

(v) Pollution from Nuclear Power Plants : It causes cancers, birth defects etc, which is life – threatening. (1)

22. Dr. B.R. Ambedkar sought reservation for dalits in educational institutions. For him, political empowerment was the only way of achieving upliftment for dalits. Dr. B.R. Ambedkar and other dalit leaders demanded separate electorates for the depressed classes in order to protect their interest and extending political power to them. Dr. B.R. Ambedkar formed the depressed classes Association in 1930 and demanded the following:

(i) To bring about political empowerment of the depressed classes. (½)

(ii) To have reserved seats in the educational institutions. (½)

(iii) He also mooted the idea of reservation for dalits which brought him in clash with Gandhi. (1)

(iv) Demanded separate electorates and bring about social justice. (1)

(v) It was with Ambedkar's constant persuasion which was eventually resolved with the Poona Pact of 1932, which provided for reserved seats in Provincial and central Legislatures for them. (1)

(vi) He also launched Kaiaram temple movement that sought entry of dalit in the Brahmin dominated temples. (1)

OR

The civil Disobedience Movement led by M.K. Gandhi, in the year 1930 was an important milestone in the history of Indian Nationalism, it began with Gandhi's famous salt march of about 240 miles from Sabarmati Ashram in Ahmedabad to the costal town of dandi in Gujarat.

(i) Civil Disobedience Movement was one of the most significant movement launched by Mahatma Gandhi where people were asked not only to refuse co–operation but also to break colonial laws. (1)

(ii) The rich peasants became enthusiastic supporters of the civil disobedience movement participating in the boycott programmes. (1)

(iii) For the rich peasants, the fight was a struggle against high revenue. (1)

(iv) The poorer peasants were not just interested in the lowering of the revenue demand but also wanted the unpaid rent to the landlords to be remitted. (1)

(v) Apprehensive of raising issues that might upset rich peasants, the congress was unwilling to support 'no rent' campaigns in most places. (1)

23. Indian trade has played a crucial role in the late nineteenth century world economy which can be explained as:

(i) Export of raw cotton from India increased from 5 % to 35 %. (½)

(ii) Indigo used for dyeing clothes was another important export for many decades. (½)

(iii) Opium shipment to china grew rapidly to become India's single largest export. (1)

(iv) Money earned through the sale of opium was used to finance its tea and other imports from china. (1)

(v) Britain had a 'Trade Surplus' with India Britain used this surplus to balance trade deficit with other countries resulting in multilateral settlement. (1)

(vi) Food grains and raw material export from India to Britain and rest of the world increased. (1)

OR

A series of changes affected the pattern of industrialization in India by the early twentieth century due to various reasons. They are

(i) Swadeshi Movement : Swadeshi and Boycott movement provided impetus to Indian industries leading to higher demand of Indian goods. (1)

(ii) Formation of Business Association : Formation of FICCI also helped them to protect their collective interest against increasing tariff. (1)

(iii) Decline of Indian Goods to China : It was due to production of cotton goods rather than yarn. (1)

(iv) Impact of World War I : World war I created a different situation where import to India declined as the British factories were producing to meet the war needs. (1)

(v) At the same time, Indian factories were called upon to supply war needs such as jute bags, clothes and shoes etc. (1)

Hence these changes resulted in creation of resilient and sustainable industrial growth to meet the domestic demand.

OR

Industrialization changed the form of urbanization in the modern period.

(v) Road transport is economical in t

(i) The early industrial cities of Britains such as Leeds and Manchester attracted large number of migrants to the textile mills set up in the late 18th century. (1)

(ii) London was a colossal city and its population expanded four–fold from 1 million to 4 million, as the Industrial revolution attracted more and more people. (1)

(iii) The city of London was a powerful magnet for migrant populations, even though it did not have large factories. (1)

(iv) Apart from the London Dock yards, five major types of industries employed large numbers: Clothing and footwear, wood and furniture, metals and engineering, printing and stationery and precision products such as surgical instruments, watches and objects of precious metals. (1)

(v) During the first world war (1914–18), London began manufacturing motor cars and electrical goods and the number of large factories increased until they accounted for nearly one–third of all jobs in the city. (1)

24. Democracy is a better form of government than other alternatives because:

(i) Promotes Equality Among Citizens: It promotes equality among people by providing equal rights for everyone. It brings social, economic and political equality among all. (1)

(ii) Enhances the Dignity of the Individual : Democracy provides rights for the protection of disadvantageous group where by dignity of every individual irrespective of any differences is upheld. (1)

(iii) Improves the quality of decision making : Decision making takes place through debate, discussion and deliberation leading to quality decision making. (1)

(iv) Provides a method to resolve conflict : Conflict and disagreement is obvious in multi–cultural society but these conflicts can be resolved through constitutional and democratic means. (1)

(v) Allows room to correct mistakes : Democracy enshrines a system of check and balance which allows timely rectification of mistakes if any. (1)

(vi) Democracy provides an accountable and responsible government. (1)

25. There are five facilities available in the Special Economic Zones developed by the central and state governments to attract foreign investment:

(i) Single window clearance for setting up of a Special Economic Zone. (1)

(ii) Exemption from Import duty. (1)

(iii) Five years tax holiday (Income Tax). (1)

(iv) Liberalizsation in labour laws and availability of skilled and semi–skilled labour forces. (1)

(v) Will connected with the network of transport and communication. (1)

SECTION D

26. (a)   (2×1=2)

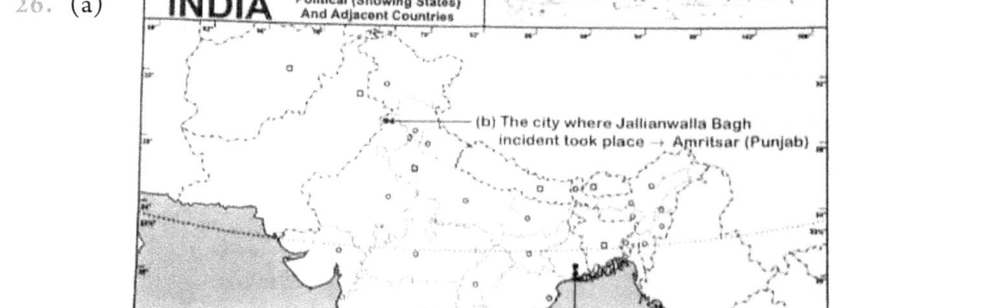

(b)   (3×1=3)

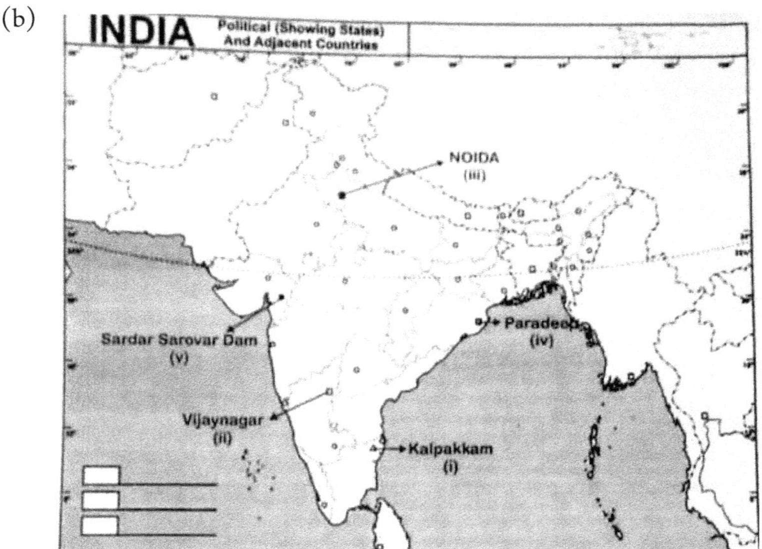

CBSE
Solved Paper 2020

Social Science
Class X

Time : 3 hrs **Maximum Marks : 80**

Read the following instructions very carefully and strictly follow them :

(i) The question paper comprises **four** Sections **A, B, C** and **D**. There are 35 questions in the question paper. **All** questions are compulsory.

(ii) **Section A** – all questions no. **1** to **20** are very short answer type questions, carrying **1 mark** each.

(iii) **Section B** – question no. **21** to **28** are short answer type questions, carrying **3 marks** each. Answer of each question should not exeed **80 words**.

(iv) **Section C** – question no. **29** to **34** are long answer type questions, carrying **5 marks** each. Answer of each question should not exceed **120 words**.

(v) **Section D** – question no. **35** is map based carrying **6 marks** with two parts **35a** from History (2 marks) and **35b** from Geography (**4 marks**).

(vi) Answer should be brief and to the point, also the above word limit be adhered to as far as possible.

(vii) There is no overall choice in the question paper. However, an internal choice has been provided in few questions. Only one of the choices in such questions have to be attempted.

(viii) Attach **MAP** along with your answer book.

(ix) In addition to this, separate instructions are given with each section and question, wherever necessary.

SECTION A

1. Name the Civil Code of 1804 which established equality before law and secured the right to property in France. (1)

2. Who among the following wrote the Vande Mataram ?
    (a) Rabindranath Tagore
    (b) Bankim Chandra Chattopadhyay
    (c) Abindranath Tagore
    (d) Dwarkanath Tagore (1)

3. Which one of the following was NOT the reason for the popularity of scientific ideas among the common people in eighteenth century Europe ?

    (a) Printing of ideas of Isaac Newton

    (b) Development of printing press

    (c) Interest of people in science and reason

    (d) Traditional aristocratic groups supported it   (1)

4. Name the two hostile groups of Second World War.   (1)

OR

    Name the two industrialists of Bombay who built huge industrial empires during nineteenth century.   (1)

5. Which among the following best signifies the idea of liberal nationalism of nineteenth century Europe ?

    (a) Emphasis on social justice

    (b) State planned socio-economic system

    (c) Freedom for individual and equality before law

    (d) Supremacy of State oriented nationalism.   (1)

6. "When France sneezes, the rest of Europe catches cold". Who among the following said this popular line ?

    (a) Guiseppe Mazzini   (b) Matternich

    (c) Otto Von Bismarck   (d) Guiseppe Garibaldi   (1)

7. Certain events are given below. Choose the appropriate chronological order :

    1. Coming of Simon Commission to India

    2. Demand of Purna Swaraj in Lahore Session of INC.

    3. Government of India Act, 1919

    4. Champaran Satyagraha

    Choose the correct option :

    (a) $3 - 2 - 4 - 1$ (b) $1 - 2 - 4 - 3$

    (c) $2 - 3 - 1 - 4$ (d) $4 - 3 - 1 - 2$ (1)

8. Complete the following table with appropriate terms in places of A and B.

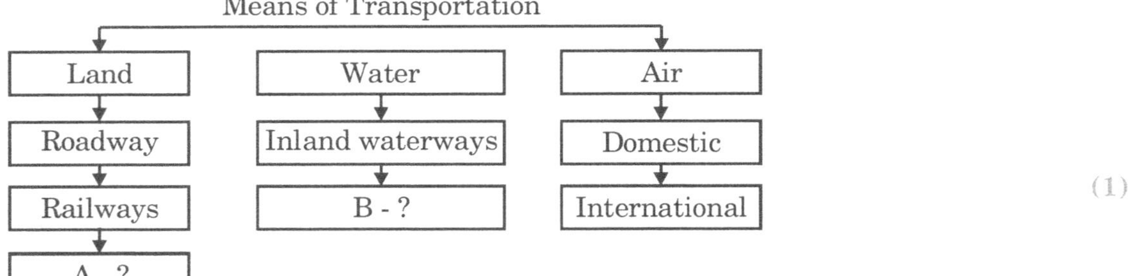

(1)

9. India has emerged as a software giant at the International level. Suggest any one way to enhance the export of information technology.   (1)

10. Business Processes Outsourcing (BPO) is an example of ______ industry in India   (1)

OR

Lime stone, silica, alumina and gypsum are the raw materials of ______ industry.   (1)

11. Read the following features of a soil and name the related soil :

(a) Develops in high rainfall area.

(b) Intense leaching process takes place.

(c) Humus content is low.   (1)

12. Write the temperature requirement of Maize crop.   (1)

OR

Write the amount of annual rainfall required for the cultivation of Wheat.   (1)

13. Read the following information and write a single term for it.

The Constitution of India provides freedom to profess and practice any religion to all its citizens. The Constitution of India prohibits discrimination on religious grounds.   (1)

14. Consider the following statements regarding language policy of Indian Federation.

(1) Hindi was identified as the official language.

(2) Besiders Hindi, there are 21 other languages recognized as scheduled languages.

(3) English can be used alone with Hindi for official purpose.

Choose the right option from the following :

(a) 1 and 3   (b) 1 and 2

(c) only 1   (d) 1, 2 and 3   (1)

15. In the question given below, there are two statements marked as Assertion (A) and Reason (R). Read the statements and choose the correct option :

Assertion (A) : Democracy is a legitimate government.

Reason (R) : Regular, free and fair elections are the spirit of democracy.

Options :

(a) Both (A) and (R) are true and (R) is the correct explanation of (A).

(b) Both (A) and (R) are incorrect.

(c) (A) is correct, but (R) is incorrect.

(d) (A) is incorrect, but (R) is correct.   (1)

16. Suggest any one way to make political parties more responsive to the people's need and demand.	(1)

OR

Suggest any one way to promote the public participation in the Political Parties for enhencing the quality of democracy.	(1)

17. Correct the following statement and rewrite it.

Removing barriers or restrictions by the government is known as Globalisation.	(1)

OR

International Monetary Fund (IMF) is an organization whose aim is to liberalise international trade.	(1)

18. Which among the following issues currency notes on behalf of the Central Government ?

(a) State Bank of India	(b) Reserve Bank of India

(c) Commercial Bank of India	(d) Union Bank of India	(1)

19. Choose the incorrect option from the following :

List I	List II
(a) Courier	(1) Tertiary Sector
(b) Fisherman	(2) Primary Sector
(c) Carpenter	(3) Primary Sector
(d) Banker	(4) Tertiary Sector

(1)

20. Define the term Per Capita income.	(1)

OR

Define the term Literacy rate.	(1)

SECTION B

21. Describe the implications of First World War on the economic and political situation of India.	(3)

OR

Describe the role of poor peasantry in the 'Civil Disobedience Movement.'	(3)

22. How had Indian trade been beneficial for the British during seventeenth century ? Explain.	(3)

OR

Why did the elite of Britain prefer handmade goods in the mid nineteenth century ? Explain.	(3)

23. "A concerted effort has to be made in order to use mineral resources in a planned and sustainable manner." Suggest and explain any three measures. (3)

24. "The pace of change in the communication sector has been rapid in modern times." Support the statement with examples. (3)

OR

"Roadways have an edge over Railways." Support the statement with examples. (3)

25. Describe the rationale behind the implementation of Decentralisation in India. (3)

26. Read the sources given below and answer the questions that follow :

Over a hundred countries of the world today claim and practice some kind of democratic politics: they have formal constitutions, they hold elections, they have parties and they guarantee rights of citizens. While these features are common to most of them, these democracies are very much different from each other in terms of their social situations, their economic achievements and their cultures. Clearly, what may be achieved or not achieved under each of these democracies will be very different.

(1) Explain the fascination for democracy amongst various countries. (1)

(2) Explain democracy on the basis of expected and actual outcome. (2)

27. Why is the tertiary sector becoming more important in India ? Explain. (3)

OR

Why is organized sector preferred by the employees ? Explain. (3)

28. Describe the significance of the Reserve Bank of India. (3)

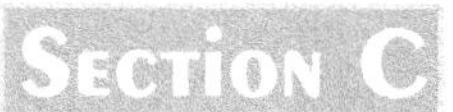

Section C

29. Read the sources given below and answer the questions that follows :

Source – 1 : Religious Reform and Public Debates

There were intense controversies between social and religious reformers and the Hindu orthodoxy over matters like widow immolation, monotheism, brahmanical priesthood and idolatry. In Bengal, as the debate developed, tracts and newspapers proliferated, circulating a variety of argument.

Source – 2 : New Forms of Publication

New literary forms also entered the world of reading lyrics, short stories, essays about social and political matters. In different ways, they reinforced the new emphasis on human lives and intimate feelings, about the political and social rules that shaped such things.

Source – 3 : Women and Print

Since social reforms and novels had already created a great interest in women's lives and emotions, there was also an interest in what women would have to say about their own lives.

Source – 1 : Religious Reform and Public Debates

(1) Evaluate how did the print shape the nature of the debate in the early nineteenth century in India.   (1)

Source – 2 : New Forms of Publication

(2) To what extent to do agree that print opened up new worlds of experience and gave a vivid sense of diversity of human lives ?   (2)

Source – 3 : Women and Print

(3) To what extent did the print culture reflect a great interest in women's lives and emotions ? Explain.   (2)

30. Explain the factors which are responsible for location of industries.   (5)

OR

Explain the ways through which the industrial pollution of fresh water can be reduced.

(5)

31. 'Communalism can take various forms in politics.' Explain.   (5)

32. Describe the necessity of political parties in democratic countries.   (5)

OR

Describe the efforts to reform political parties in India.   (5)

33. "The impact of globalization has not been uniform." Explain with examples.   (5)

34. Why is sustainability important for development ? Explain.   (5)

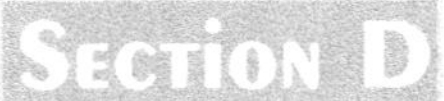

(MAP BASED QUESTION)

35. (a) Two places A and B are marked on the given political outline map of India. Identify them and write their correct names on the lines drawn near them.

(A) The place where Indian National Congress Session was held.

(B) The place where Indigo Planters organized Satyagraha.   (2)

(b) On the same outline map of India, locate and label any four of the following with appropriate symbols :

    (i)   Haldia   –   Major Sea Port

    (ii) Mohali   –   Software Technology Park

    (iii) Vijayanagar   –   Iron and Steel Industrial Centre

    (iv) Naraura   –   Nuclear Power Plant

    (v) Tehri   –   Dam

    (vi) Thiruvananthapuram   –   International Airport   (4)

Solution

SECTION A

1. The Napoleonic code   (1)

2. (b) Bankim chandra chattopadhyay   (1)

3. (d) Traditional Aristocratic groups supported it.   (1)

4. The two hostile groups of second world war were –

   The Central Powers and

   The Allies   (1)

   OR

   Purshottandas Thakurdas and G.D Birla

                                                                           (1)

5. Freedom for individual and equality before law.   (1)

6. Matternich   (1)

7. 4 – 3 – 1– 2   (1)

8. A- pipelines   (½)

   B- Overseas waterways   (½)

9. International trade   (1)

10. Information Technology and Electronics Industry   (1)

    OR

    Cement Industry   (1)

11. (a) Forest soils

    (b) Laterite soil

    (c) Forest soils   (1)

12. Between 21°C to 27°C   (1)

    OR

    50 to 75 cm   (1)

13. Secularism   (1)

14. (d) 1, 2 and 3   (1)

15. (a) Both (A) and (R) are true and (R) is the correct explanation of (A).   (1)

16. A law should be made to regulate the internal affairs of political parties. It should be made compulsory for political parties to maintain a record of its members.   (1)

OR

One way to promote public participation in political parties is that those people who want this join political parties. (1)

17. Incorrect: Removing barriers on restriction by the government is known as <u>Globalisation</u>.

Correct: Removing barriers or restrictions by the government is known as <u>liberalisation</u>. (1)

OR

Incorrect : International Monetary Fund (IME) is an organisation whose aim is to liberalise International Trade

Correct: World Trade Organisation (WTO) is an organisation whose aim is to liberalise International Trade. (1)

18. (b) Reserve Bank of India (1)

19. (c) Carpenter   (3) Primary sector (1)

20. When the total income of the country is divided by the total population is called as per capita income. (1)

OR

It measures the proportion of literate population in the 7 and above age group.

(1)

Section B

21. The war created a new economic and political situation.

- It led to a huge increase in defence expenditure which was financed by war loans and increasing taxes: customs duties were raised and income tax introduced. (1)

- Through the war years prices increased- doubling between 1913 and 1918, leading to extreme hardship for the common people. (1)

- Villages were called upon to supply soldiers.

- Then in 1920-21 and 1918-19, crops failed in many parts of India, resulting in famine.

- This was accompanied by an influenga epidemic. (1)

OR

The poor peasantry were not just interested in the covering of the revenue demand.

- Many of them were small tenants cultivating land they had rented from landlords. (1)

- As the Depression continued and cash incomes durindeed, the small tenants found it difficult be pay their rent.

- They wanted the unpaid rent to the landlord to be remmitted. They joined a variety of radical movements. (1)

- Apprehensive of raising issues that might upset the rich peasants and landeords, the congress was unwilling to support 'no rent'campaigns in most places. (1)

22. Trade with India was greatly beneficial to the Britishers in 17th century.

   (i) India exported products like Cotton, Silk, Indigo which was in high demand in Britain.

   (1)

   (ii) India was the source of high value products like spices for Britain. (1)

   (iii) All these items were in demand in Britain and their availability at cheaper rate from India enhanced the quality of life for the Britishers.

   (1)

OR

This is because :

   (i) The upper classes preferred the expensive hand made products for their exclusiveness, which were not shared by all. (1)

   (ii) Hand made products were better finished, individually produced and designed carefully. (1)

   (iii) Handmade products came to symbolise refinement and class. (1)

23. A concerted effort has to be made in order to use our mineral resources in a planned and sustainable manner.

   • Improved technologies need to the constantly evolved to allow the extraction of minerals at low cost and to allow use of low grade ores at low costs. (1)

   • Another way can be recycling the metals and using scrap metals to avoid wastage. (1)

   • Substitutes can be used instead of metals. This would lead to conservation of our mineral resources for the future. (1)

24. The pace of change in the communication sector has been rapid in

   • Long distance communication is now easier without pysical movement of the communicator or receiver. (1)

   • Personal communication and mass communication including television press etc.are the major means of communication. (1)

   • The Indian postal network is the largest in the world. It handles parcels as well as personal written communications. (1)

OR

Roadways have an edge over railways.

   • Construction cost of roadways is much lower than railways.

   • Roads can transeverse comparitively more dissected and undulating topography. (1)

   • Roads can negotiate higher gradients of slopes.

   • Road transport is economical in transportation of few persons and relatively smaller amount of goods over short distances. (1)

   • It also provides door- to- door service.

   • Road transport acts as a link between other modes of transportation. (1)

25. The basic idea behind decentralisation is that there are a large number of problems and issues which are best settled at the local level. (1)

   • People also have better ideas on where to spend money and how to manage things more efficiently. (1)

   • At the local level, it is possible for the people to directly participate in decision making. This helps to inculcate a habit of democratic participation. (1)

26.1 Over a hundred countries of the world today claim and practice some kind of democratic politics. They have formal constitutions, they hold elections, they have parties and the guarantee rights to citizens. (1)

   2. Democracy can be measured on the following basis :

   (i)   Accountable, responsive and legitimate government.

   (ii) Economic growth and development. (1)

   (iii) Reduction of inequality and poverty.

   (iv) Dignity and freedom of citizens. (1)

27. In any country several services like hospitals, educational institutions, police stations etc., are considered as basic services. In a developing country the government has to take responsibility for the provision of these services. (1)

   • The development of agriculture and industry leads to the development of services such as transport, trade, storage etc. Greater the development of primary and secondary sectors, more would be the demand for such services. (1)

   • As income levels rise, certain sections of people start demanding many more services like eating outs, tourism, shopping, private hospitals etc. (1)

OR

Organised sector is preferred by the employees because it gives the following advantages over unorganised sector.

   • It is registered with the Government.

   • There are fixed working hours. (1)

   • Employees get fixed salary on a fixed date every month. (1)

   • Salary is not deducted for holidays.

   • There are other facilities like provident fund, maternity leave and paid leave etc. (1)

28. The Reserve Bank of India supervises the functioning of formal sources of credit.

   • The RBI monitors the banks in actually maintaining cash balance. (1)

   • The RBI ensures that banks gives loans not just to profit-making businessmen and traders, but also to small cultivater, small industrialists, the small borrowers etc. (1)

   • Periodically, banks have to submit information to the RBI on how much they are lending, to whom, at what interest rate, etc. (1)

Section C

29.1 From the early nineteenth century there were intense debates aroud religious issues. Some criticised existing practices and campaigned for reform, while others countered the arguments of reformers. (1)

2 Print culture was not just a development, a new way of producing books; it transformed the lives of people, changing their relationship to information and knowledge and with institutions and authorities. It influenced popular perceptions and opened up new ways of looking at things. (2)

3. Lives and feeling of woman began to be written in particularly vivid and intense ways.

- Liberal husbands and fathers began educating their womanfolk at home, and sent them to schools. (1)

- Many journals began carrying writing by women, and explained why women should be educated. (1)

30. Industrial locations are complex in nature.

- They are influenced by availability of -

1. Raw material
2. Labour
3. Capital
4. Power
5. Market (2½)

- Manufacturing activity tends to locate at the most appropriate place where all the factors of industrial location are either available or can be arranged at low cost. (1)

- Sometimes, industries are located in or near the cities. Because cities provide markets and also provide services such as insurance, transport, labour etc. to the industry. (1½)

OR

Some suggestions are :-

- Minimising use water for processing by reusing and recycling it in two or more successive stages. (1)

- Harvesting of rainwater to meet water requirements. (1)

- Treating hot water and effluants before releasing them in rivers and ponds. Treatment of industrial effluents can be done in three phases:

  1. Primary treatment by mechanical means. (1)

  2. Secondary treatment by biological process. (1)

  3. Tertiary treatment by biological, chemical and physical means. This involves recycling of wastewater. (1)

31. The most common expression of communalism is in everyday beliefs. These routinely involve religious prejudices, stereotypes of religious communities and belief in the superiority of one's religion over other religions. (2)

- A communal mind often leads to a quest for political dominance of one's own religious community. For those belonging to majority community, this takes the form of majoritarian dominance. (1)

- Political mobilisation on religious lines is another frequent form of communalism. (1)

- Sometimes communalism takes its most ugly form of communal violence, riots and massacre. (1)

32. Political parties are necessary because they perform the following functions-

- Parties contest elections. (1)

- Parties put forward different policies and programmes and the voters choose from them. (1)

- Parties play a decisive role in making laws for a country. (1)

- Parties form and run governments. (1)

- Parties shape public opinion. (1)

OR

The constitution was amended to prevent elected MLAs and MPs from changing parties.

- This was done because many elected representatives were indulging in defection in order to become ministers or for cash rewards. (2)

- The supreme court passed an order to reduce the influence of money and criminals. (1½)

- The election commission passed an order making it necessary for political parties to hold their organisational elections and file their income tax returns. (1½)

33. The impact of globalization has not been uniform because :

(a) It has largely enhanced life style of well off in society as MNC's mostly focused on cell phones, automobiles, electronics, soft drinks fast food or services such as banking in urban areas. (½)

(b) New jobs have been created in these sectors. (½)

(c) Local companies supplying raw materials for these industries also prospered. (½)

(d) Globalisation has also created new opportunities for companies providing services, particularly those involving it, call centers. (1)

Globalisation also brought its negative impact in terms of :

(a) Smaller businesses were impacted badly as they lost their market share due to rising competition and cheaper products. (1)

(b) Consumers started opting for cheaper products against quality products as technology upgrades become frequent and shelf life of products decreased. (1)

(c) Unskilled labours turned jobless as small scaled industries closed down. (½)

34. • It takes care of the needs of the future generation. (1)

    • It promotes efficient use of natural resources. (1)

    • It lays emphasis on equality of life. (1)

    • It suggests measures for growth and development effectively (1)

    • It ensures equal distribution of resources to everyone. (1)

Section D

35. (a) (A) Calcutta

       (B) Champaran (2)

   (b) (4)

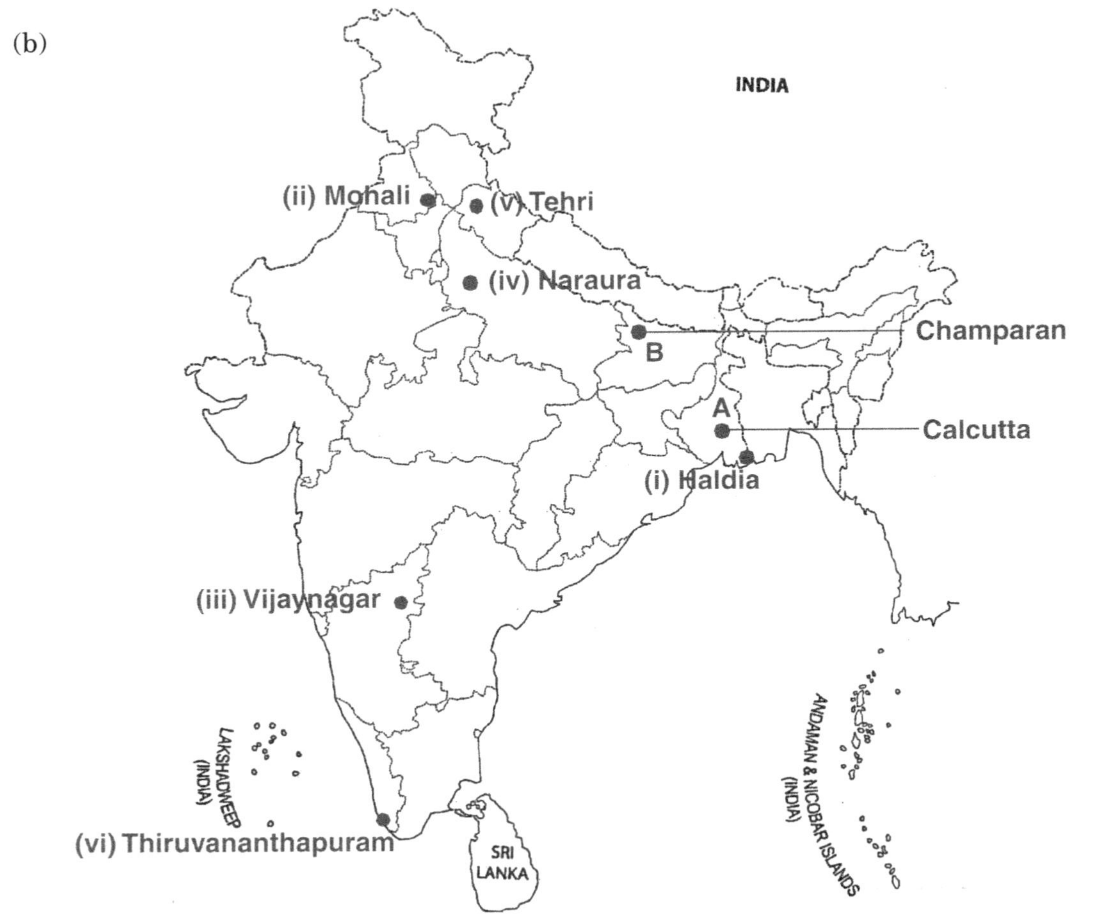

www.ingramcontent.com/pod-product-compliance
Lightning Source LLC
LaVergne TN
LVHW080619200726
843509LV00007B/349